Praise for *Lead Boldly*

"With *Lead Boldly*, Robert F. Smith captures the essence of true leadership in complex times. This is a book about leadership, yes, but it is also about humanity and the power of one individual to inspire change. It blends wisdom, vision, and courage into a guide for those who dare to challenge the status quo and create spaces of equity and opportunity."

—SERENA WILLIAMS, champion professional tennis player

"*Lead Boldly* is a masterclass in leadership with heart and purpose. Robert F. Smith takes readers on a poignant journey of courage, resilience, and transformational vision. This book serves as an invaluable resource for those committed to building a more inclusive future."

—DARREN WALKER, president of the Ford Foundation

"Inspired by the prophetic words of Dr. King, visionary business leader and history-making philanthropist Robert Smith outlines in clear and compelling prose his brilliant prescriptions for closing the gap between 'the Dream' and the reality of racial and economic relations in our country today. *Lead Boldly*—deeply anchored in the Black tradition and rooted in family and community—is interwoven with profoundly moving personal experiences that thoroughly ground Smith's clear, compelling, and original program for delivering on King's urgent plea for economic justice, more than sixty years after Smith attended the March on Washington as a child with his parents. Anyone reading this exciting and urgently needed book will be enlightened, feel inspired, and be eager to engage in 'the work' needed to make Dr. King's dream, at long last, a reality for all Americans. *Lead Boldly* is a timely, original, and heroic intervention at a time of crisis in race relations in our country, written by the most successful entrepreneur in African American history and a genuine thought leader for our times."

—HENRY LOUIS GATES JR., Alphonse Fletcher University
      Professor, Harvard University

"Robert F. Smith's *Lead Boldly* is nothing short of essential reading. Drawing on the timeless lessons of Dr. Martin Luther King Jr., this book offers profound leadership insights that resonate deeply in today's world. Smith's commitment to racial reconciliation and inclusion shines through every page, making it a vital blueprint for leaders seeking to create meaningful change. This is not just a book for our time—it's a gift for future generations."

—REV. AL SHARPTON, founder and president of National Action Network

"*Lead Boldly* is more than a reflection on the legacy of Dr. King—it's a call to action for leaders to embody his principles in practical, transformative ways. Robert masterfully bridges the lessons of the past with the challenges of today, making this a must-read for anyone committed to leading with impact."

—RASHAD BILAL AND TROY MILLINGS, cocreators of *Earn
      Your Leisure*

"*Lead Boldly* is a powerful call to action for leaders everywhere, urging them to embrace the responsibility of shaping a more just and equitable world. Robert F. Smith masterfully blends the wisdom, vision, and courage of Dr. Martin Luther King Jr. into a guide for those who dare to challenge the status quo and create spaces of opportunity. Both inspiring and pragmatic, this book offers a clear road map for those seeking to make a lasting impact. More than just a leadership guide, *Lead Boldly* is a testament to how Robert has developed his career and lived his life—with purpose, conviction, and an unwavering commitment to justice. In a time when the call to build the Beloved Community is more urgent than ever, this book serves as a North Star, illuminating the path toward a future rooted in equity, empowerment, and transformative leadership. It is, at its core, a blueprint for those who aspire to relevance and seek to leave a meaningful legacy."

—REV. DR. W. FRANKLYN RICHARDSON, bestselling author
of *Witness to Grace*; senior pastor of Grace Baptist Church; chairman, National Action Network

"True leadership is about more than success—it is about courage, healing, and an unwavering commitment to our shared humanity. In *Lead Boldly*, Robert F. Smith offers a blueprint for a new generation of leaders who understand that justice and belonging are essential for building the world we want for all our children and that the strength of a nation lies in its ability to uplift all people. His words inspire and challenge us to dismantle barriers, reach across divides, and move forward together toward a future where every child and community can reach their full potential."

—LA JUNE MONTGOMERY TABRON, president and CEO,
W. K. Kellogg Foundation; author of *How We Heal*

"*Lead Boldly* is a must-read for leaders in today's uncertain times. Robert Smith has expertly curated speeches of Dr. Martin Luther King Jr., America's most transformative leader and prophetic voice, into seven profound leadership lessons grounded in the ethical, spiritual, and intellectual demands of leading in our time. It is a must-read for all leaders and change agents in organizations everywhere, regardless of industry or sector. It will certainly be required reading in my course on leadership."

—DAVID A. THOMAS, twelfth president, Morehouse College; Naylor Fitzhugh Professor Emeritus, Harvard University

"This book is about leadership, yes, but it is also about humanity and the power of one individual to inspire change. Grounded in readings of some of Dr. Martin Luther King Jr.'s greatest speeches, Robert F. Smith's *Lead Boldly* is a tour de force, challenging each of us to rise to the occasion with integrity and purpose. It is a gift to all who envision a brighter tomorrow."

—MICHAEL LOMAX, president and CEO, UNCF; champion for Black higher education and equity in America

Lead Boldly

Lead Boldly

Seven Principles
from Dr. Martin Luther King Jr.

With Insights from
ROBERT F. SMITH

Foreword by REV. DR. BERNICE A. KING

Published in partnership with

An Imprint of HarperCollins*Publishers*

An Imprint of HarperCollins

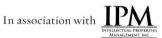

Contents

Foreword

ead Boldly is a personal reflection of how Robert F. Smith was inspired by my father, Rev. Dr. Martin Luther King Jr., and his leadership and desire to build the "Beloved Community." It helped propel Robert to become one of America's premier business leaders. My father believed earnestly in the Beloved Community. Although he preached passionately about love, peace, hope, equality, and brotherhood, for him, all these roads lead to the Beloved Community. My father offered a deeper meaning than the ordinary definitions of *beloved* and *community.*

For him, the Beloved Community was a place without poverty, racism, and war. How could poverty proliferate in a community where each person loved each other; where being our brother's keeper was a blessing not a burden; where sharing resources was more important than hoarding them? How could racism ever raise its ugly head in a place where each person viewed themselves equal to each other; a community based on a belief that God created everyone equally? Such a Beloved Community has no need for war because genuine conflicts can be resolved through nonviolence. I am reminded of Philippians 2:3–4: "Do nothing out of selfish ambition or vain conceit. Rather, in humility value others above yourselves, not looking to your own interests but each of you to the interest of others." My father said, "I can't be all I ought to be, if you are not all you ought to be" and "We are caught in an inescapable network of mutuality, tied in a single garment of destiny. What effects one directly, affects all indirectly."

For my father, nonviolence, as the pathway to the Beloved Community, was not simply the absence of violence; it was the presence of peace and justice. Nonviolence was more than an activist methodology; it was a way of living that could and should be applied to all aspects of life. For him, violence came in many forms, not just physical violence. For instance, the lack of adequate healthcare; limited access to proper education; the lack of economic opportunities and a means of earning a sufficient income to feed your family. All of these were different forms of violence inflicted upon the less fortunate and less powerful.

As a leader, Robert was also heavily influenced by my father's poignant discussions of America as a country where Black Americans lacked equity, and whose lived experience varied greatly from that of many of their white counterparts. My father would describe this condition as "the Two Americas," and for Robert it was a testament to his own life experiences. While God created us all equal, not all Americans have shared an equal path as citizens of this country. For every child that awakes in a warm and loving home, there is a child who wakes up in the desperate confines of a homeless shelter. For every child that rises to the smell of freshly cooked breakfast, there is a child awakened by a growling stomach and uncertainty of when they will have their next meal. For every child that attends a well-funded and adequately supplied suburban school, there is a child who attends an underfunded inner-city school lacking the most basic educational supplies. These are also forms of violence. When that inner-city schoolchild doesn't achieve as well as that suburban schoolchild, the inner-city child is often told they should simply try harder, which implies that their plight is due to their own lack of effort.

My father yearned for the day when two seeds planted in equally nurturing soil could flourish; when one seed wasn't forced to become that proverbial "rose that grew from concrete." He believed in a Beloved Community where all citizens were given equal opportunities to develop; where all people could provide their unique talents and skills toward uplifting the whole community, making life better for all. Imagine the force of will exerted if all well-intentioned people worldwide were pulling in the same direction. This is the power of the Beloved Community.

Inequality and all forms of segregation are obstacles to creating a Beloved Community. For our country and world to be all it should be, we need all hands on deck. Attempting to relegate individuals to a lesser role in society because of their race, ethnicity, or religious identity is beyond dangerous. It is tantamount to allowing water to enter only one side of the *Titanic* and actually thinking that the other side will not be affected. My father said it best: "We must learn to live together as brothers, or we will be forced to perish together as fools."

Robert F. Smith is not only a noted titan in the business community but also a student of my father's life work. As you read this book, lean in with him as he recalls several of my father's speeches and sermons, then shares how they helped shape his life's journey.

—Rev. Dr. Bernice A. King

Dr. King waves to the crowd on the Mall following his speech at the March on Washington for Jobs and Freedom, Washington, DC, August 28, 1963.

Hulton Archive / Getty Images

CHAPTER

1

Let Freedom Ring from the Snow-Capped Rockies

"I Have a Dream"

I am happy to join with you today in what will go down in history as the greatest demonstration for freedom in the history of our nation.

Fivescore years ago, a great American, in whose symbolic shadow we stand today, signed the Emancipation Proclamation. This momentous decree came as a great beacon light of hope to millions of Negro slaves who had been seared in the flames of withering injustice. It came as a joyous daybreak to end the long night of their captivity.

But one hundred years later, the Negro still is not free; one hundred years later, the life of the Negro is still sadly crippled by the manacles of segregation and the chains of discrimination; one hundred years later, the Negro lives on a lonely island of poverty in the midst of a vast ocean of material prosperity; one hundred years later, the Negro is still languished in the corners of American society and finds himself in exile in his own land.

So we've come here today to dramatize a shameful condition. In a sense we've come to our nation's capital to cash a check. When the architects of our republic wrote the magnificent words of the Constitution and the Declaration of Independence, they were signing a promissory note to which every American was to fall heir. This note was the promise that all men, yes, Black men as well as white men, would be guaranteed the unalienable rights of life, liberty, and the pursuit of happiness.

It is obvious today that America has defaulted on this promissory note in so far as her citizens of color are concerned. Instead of honoring this sacred obligation, America has given the Negro people a bad check; a check which has come back marked "insufficient funds." We refuse to believe that there are insufficient funds in the great vaults of opportunity of this nation. And so we've come to cash this check, a check that will give us upon demand the riches of freedom and the security of justice.

We have also come to this hallowed spot to remind America of the fierce urgency of now. This is no time to engage in the luxury of cooling off or to take the tranquilizing drug of gradualism. Now is the time to make real the promises of democracy; now is the time to rise from the dark and desolate valley of segregation to the sunlit path of racial justice; now is the time to lift our nation from the quicksands of racial injustice to the solid rock of brotherhood; now is the time to make justice a reality for all God's children. It would be fatal for the nation to overlook the urgency of the moment. This sweltering summer of the Negro's legitimate discontent will not pass until there is an invigorating autumn of freedom and equality.

Nineteen sixty-three is not an end, but a beginning. And those who hope that the Negro needed to blow off steam and will now be content, will have a rude awakening if the nation returns to business as usual.

There will be neither rest nor tranquility in America until the Negro is granted his citizenship rights. The whirlwinds of revolt will continue to shake the foundations of our nation until the bright day of justice emerges.

But there is something that I must say to my people, who stand on the warm threshold which leads into the palace of justice. In the process of gaining our rightful place we must not be guilty of wrongful deeds.

Let us not seek to satisfy our thirst for freedom by drinking from the cup of bitterness and hatred. We must forever conduct our struggle on the high plane of dignity and discipline. We must not allow our creative protest to degenerate into physical violence. Again and again we must rise to the majestic heights of meeting physical force with soul force.

The marvelous new militancy which has engulfed the Negro community must not lead us to a distrust of all white people, for many of our white brothers, as evidenced by their presence here today, have come to realize that their destiny is tied up with our destiny and they have come to realize that their freedom is inextricably bound to our freedom. This offense we share mounted to storm the battlements of injustice must be carried forth by a biracial army. We cannot walk alone.

And as we walk, we must make the pledge that we shall always march ahead. We cannot turn back. There are those who are asking the devotees of civil rights, "When will you be satisfied?" We can never be satisfied as long as the Negro is the victim of the unspeakable horrors of police brutality.

We can never be satisfied as long as our bodies, heavy with fatigue of travel, cannot gain lodging in the motels of the highways and the hotels of the cities. We cannot be satisfied as long as the Negro's basic mobility is from a smaller ghetto to a larger one.

We can never be satisfied as long as our children are stripped of their selfhood and robbed of their dignity by signs stating "for whites only." We cannot be satisfied as long as a Negro in Mississippi cannot vote and a Negro in New York believes he has nothing for which to vote. No, we are not satisfied, and we will not be satisfied until justice rolls down like waters and righteousness like a mighty stream.

I am not unmindful that some of you have come here out of excessive trials and tribulation. Some of you have come fresh from narrow jail cells. Some of you have come from areas where your quest for freedom left you battered by the storms of persecution and staggered by the winds of police brutality. You have been the veterans of creative suffering. Continue to work with the faith that unearned suffering is redemptive.

Go back to Mississippi; go back to Alabama; go back to South Carolina; go back to Georgia; go back to Louisiana; go back to the slums and ghettos of the Northern cities, knowing that somehow this situation can and will be changed. Let us not wallow in the valley of despair.

So I say to you, my friends, that even though we must face the difficulties of today and tomorrow, I still have a dream. It is a dream deeply rooted in the American dream that one day this nation will rise up and live out the true meaning of its creed—we hold these truths to be self-evident, that all men are created equal.

I have a dream that one day on the red hills of Georgia, sons of former slaves and sons of former slave-owners will be able to sit down together at the table of brotherhood.

I have a dream that one day, even the state of Mississippi, a state sweltering with the heat of injustice, sweltering with the heat of oppression, will be transformed into an oasis of freedom and justice.

I have a dream my four little children will one day live in a nation where they will not be judged by the color of their skin but by content of their character. I have a dream today!

I have a dream that one day, down in Alabama, with its vicious racists, with its governor having his lips dripping with the words of interposition and nullification, that one day, right there in Alabama, little Black boys and Black girls will be able to join hands with little white boys and white girls as sisters and brothers. I have a dream today!

I have a dream that one day every valley shall be exalted, every hill and mountain shall be made low, the rough places shall be made plain, and the crooked places shall be made straight and the glory of the Lord will be revealed and all flesh shall see it together.

This is our hope. This is the faith that I go back to the South with.

With this faith we will be able to hew out of the mountain of despair a stone of hope. With this faith we will be able to transform the jangling discords of our nation into a beautiful symphony of brotherhood.

With this faith we will be able to work together, to pray together, to struggle together, to go to jail together, to stand up for freedom together, knowing that we will be free one day. This will be the day when all of God's children will be able to sing with new meaning—"my country 'tis of thee; sweet land of liberty; of thee I sing; land where my fathers died, land of the pilgrim's pride; from every mountainside, let freedom ring"—and if America is to be a great nation, this must become true.

So let freedom ring from the prodigious hilltops of New Hampshire.

Let freedom ring from the mighty mountains of New York.

Let freedom ring from the heightening Alleghenies of Pennsylvania.

Let freedom ring from the snow-capped Rockies of Colorado.

Let freedom ring from the curvaceous slopes of California.

But not only that.

Let freedom ring from Stone Mountain of Georgia.

Let freedom ring from Lookout Mountain of Tennessee.

Let freedom ring from every hill and molehill in Mississippi, from every mountainside, let freedom ring.

And when we allow freedom to ring, when we let it ring from every village and hamlet, from every state and city, we will be able to speed up that day when all of God's children—Black men and white men, Jews and Gentiles, Catholics and Protestants—will be able to join hands and sing in the words of the old Negro spiritual, "Free at last, free at last; thank God Almighty, we are free at last."

—Dr. Martin Luther King Jr.

August 28, 1963, Lincoln Memorial, Washington, DC

Dr. King's "I Have a Dream" speech on August 28, 1963, is iconic, not only for its significance to the civil rights movement but also for its emphasis on economic justice. One of King's major themes is the unpaid debt owed to African Americans since the Emancipation Proclamation a century before, as well as the harsh racial economic disparities in America. I was there as a baby on the National Mall with my mother when King delivered his iconic address. Dr. King's life and his teachings have been a guiding force throughout my life, inspiring me to see the world as it is, with its problems, but also to imagine a fairer and more just world and to work toward making it a reality.

When Dr. Martin Luther King Jr. delivered his world-changing "I Have a Dream" speech on the National Mall in 1963, my family was among the hundreds of thousands of souls who had gathered to hear him speak. We were there at the March on Washington for Jobs and Freedom. It was a warm day in August as we stood among men, women, and children in their Sunday best while Dr. King's baritone voice boomed through the loudspeakers. We were second-class citizens in the epoch of Jim Crow, and Dr. King implored America to make good on its promise of justice for all. "We've come to our nation's capital to cash a check," he rang out.

I was just nine months old then. As I grew older, the stories my family told me about that day and how we got to Washington made a lasting impression. Their memories became mine, entwined in the tapestry of my identity.

To get to the March, my parents and aunt brought my brother and me on a 1,700-mile drive through dry Alpine heat from our home in northeast Denver to Washington, DC. The days-long voyage was mostly along US Route 36, down from the Rockies, through the rolling farmland and small towns of the Midwest. The scenery outside the car windows was so picturesque one could momentarily forget the perilous realities of cross-country travel for Black families in those uncertain times. In the 1960s, interstate travel was dangerous for people like us. Just a few months before our journey, a Ku Klux Klan member reportedly shot and killed a white civil rights activist named William Moore as he walked along a highway in Tennessee.

My parents were educators. My mother, Sylvia Smith, used her keen intellect to plot our course. She relied on a wide range of resources—*The Negro Motorist Green Book*, advice from elders, and grapevine whispers—to find the few hotels and motor lodges that served Black families. We packed lunches and brought pickle jars to use as makeshift bathrooms since the color of our skin precluded us from accessing lunch counters or public restrooms.

In that segregated world, Black Americans lived in what Dr. King called "the other America." Our job opportunities and living standards were dwarfed by those of whites. We were barred from public bathrooms, restaurants, schools, trains, and buses. Redlining constricted where and if we could buy a home. Many of those forms of Jim Crow apartheid fell in the years after the March, with the passage of the Civil Rights Act in 1964 and the Voting Rights Act the following year. But the two Americas endured racist systems that persist and respawn, restraining African Americans to this day. Even after those groundbreaking pieces of legislation, Black people had limited access to the opportunities created by the expansion of the American economy. This manifested as high unemployment, lesser-resourced schools, and constrained access to capital, which has ballooned the wealth gap between African Americans and white Americans.

I felt this personally. The Denver neighborhood where I grew up lacked a supermarket and bank. For my parents and their neighbors, getting a loan or healthy food required a car trip to a white area of town where we might not be welcome. Access to capital, nutritious food, and other resources have often been structurally out of reach for many African Americans, perpetuating gaps that persist today in business formation, family wealth, health outcomes, and lifespan.

Thanks to Dr. King and the many thousands who marched with him, I am part of the first generation in my family to have enjoyed all my rights. But sixty years after my mother took me to Washington, many African Americans still have yet to experience the full promise of America. My neighborhood in Denver still doesn't have a supermarket, and the one bank branch is rarely open. Decades later, my neighborhood—and many others—remain in the "other America."

This is a large part of what motivates my work to ensure that more people have equitable access to education, and general-purpose technologies like broadband and AI needed to connect their hard work and aspirations with their societal station.

On our trip to Washington, during one of our pit stops in Kansas, the owner of the humble hotel where my mother had booked a room took one look at the color of our skin and refused to take us in. With no alternative, we spent the night in a YWCA. Per facility rules, my dad couldn't lodge in the room with us, so he slept in the car. Incidents like these serve as reminders of why the civil rights struggle and Dr. King's leadership were paramount.

I sometimes wonder what my father, who had recently graduated with his master's in education from Denver University, thought and felt as he slept in the car that night, separated both from the dignity of proper shelter and from his loved ones. I also wonder what thoughts and emotions raced through my young mother's mind when we finally arrived in Washington after days of similar ordeals. When she stood amid the exuberant throngs, cradling her babies, I imagine she felt anxious and hopeful. Like many who had journeyed, she hoped to hear about equal rights, jobs, and opportunities. Did her heart steady at the resonant refrain of "I have a dream . . . that one day this nation will rise up and live out the true meaning of its creed—we hold these truths to be self-evident, that all men are created equal"?

Dr. King ingeniously opened his speech by reminding the audience that the March took place one hundred years after the end of slavery: "Fivescore years ago, a great American, in whose symbolic shadow we stand today, signed the Emancipation Proclamation . . . But one hundred years later, the Negro still is not free."

After more than two centuries of enslavement and deprivation—an era in which Frederick Douglass described every enslaved person as being "robbed, by his master, of all his earnings, above what is required for his bare physical necessity"—African Americans first began to grasp at the greatest wealth-building opportunity this country has ever known: land ownership. In 1865, the Freedmen's Bureau was supposed to distribute 850,000 acres of land to the newly emancipated. That program was canceled and replaced with the Freedman's

Savings Bank, a central depository institution for Black people. The head of the Treasury, George S. Boutwell, put an all-white board in charge of the bank. However, instead of being fiduciaries of the deposits of African Americans, the board members used the bank's assets to make risky investments and give loans to their friends. In 1874, the bank began to go bust due to mismanagement and fraud, jeopardizing the savings of African Americans. In the last days of the Freedman's Bank, Frederick Douglass was brought on as the head of the bank but found it beyond repair. There would be no bailout for the Freedman's Bank or its depositors, primarily Black people. Instead, it was allowed to fail and to wipe the Black depositors out. Douglass lamented that the bank had been "the black man's cow, but the white man's milk."

This wasn't an isolated instance. The first wave of wealth creation in America in the eighteenth and nineteenth centuries was generated in agriculture by producing cash crops like tobacco, rice, sugar, and cotton. Enslaved Black farmers generated millions in profits for plantation owners but did not reap the bounty of their labor.

The second wave of wealth generation occurred in the nineteenth and twentieth centuries through the accumulation and appreciation of land. This boom benefitted many Americans but mostly excluded Black people through the Freedman's Bank's failings, redlining, and a vast array of other racist practices.

In America's third wave of wealth generation, the Industrial

Revolution, Black people again participated as laborers. Still, they were rarely allowed to own factories or production facilities.

Today, in a fourth wave of wealth creation through an investment boom and the transformative power of technology, it is essential for African Americans to fully participate, not just as laborers but as asset owners.

DR. KING'S VISION FOR ECONOMIC justice resonates most with me. Seventy years after the end of the Civil War, in 1935, when the New Deal legislation began to be put into law, the bills were designed to disproportionally exclude African Americans, in part to appease the Southern coalition of the Democratic party. The 1935 Social Security Act excluded domestic and farm workers (more than two-thirds of Black workers) from receiving benefits, while the Servicemen's Readjustment Act of 1944, also known as the GI Bill, created administrative obstacles to Black veterans accessing its benefits. A 2022 study by Brandeis University found that the cash value of the benefits received by African American recipients of the GI Bill was 30 to 60 percent less than that of whites.

A rhetorical device in Dr. King's iconic speech resonates with me today: the extended metaphor of a debt. With eloquence, he employed the image of an outstanding check as a powerful symbol of America's failure to fulfill its self-evident promise of equality for all. He proclaimed, "We've come to our nation's capital to cash a check." He points out that instead of honoring this sacred obligation, America has issued a bad check—a check returned and marked "insufficient funds." Embedded within the fabric of this image is a recognition of the economic condition of Black Americans. Dr. King observed that "the Negro lives on a lonely island of poverty in the midst of a vast ocean of material prosperity." He called attention to the economic inequalities that Black people faced. His closing words were urgent and hopeful: "We refuse to believe that there are insufficient funds in the great vaults of opportunity of this nation. And so we've come to cash this check, a check that will give us upon demand the riches of freedom and the security of justice."

Economic justice is an overlooked aspect of Martin Luther King Jr.'s mission. His desire was for African Americans to have civil rights *and* economic opportunity. The March was for "Jobs and Freedom." This is what guides my mission as well. His vision for economic justice has been a driving force in my work to empower others. The call for liberation does not cease with racial harmony. It requires that all Americans—in this case, Black Americans—be able to better themselves through education, business formation, wealth creation, and the opportunity to participate in the Fourth Industrial Revolution (the modern tech boom) and to finally transcend the barriers erected and perpetuated to hold them down.

A FEW MONTHS AFTER his speech, Dr. King's eloquence was pressed onto vinyl as an album.

That record became a soundtrack of my childhood, on an eternal loop on neighbors' and shopkeepers' record players. I remember standing in line at the barbershop and hearing Dr. King's "I Have a Dream" speech crackling over the speakers while I waited to get my hair cut. By the time I reached adolescence, I had listened to this speech hundreds of times.

One line stuck with me: "Let freedom ring." The melodic quality of those words still resonates sweetly in my ears. When he proclaimed, "Let freedom ring from the snow-capped Rockies," it was as if he were speaking directly to my community in northeast Denver. But what did "Let freedom ring" indeed mean? What did freedom sound like? What did it look like? What does freedom mean to you?

My family's journey to the March on Washington and Dr. King's work and legacy ingrained in me the importance of the fight for racial justice. My parents were willing to suffer the injustices of whites-only establishments along the highways to Washington to be there for Dr. King's most important address. In doing so, they modeled persistence for me, a lesson Dr. King would echo on the vinyl record that played throughout my childhood. The line from his speech, "As we walk, we must make the pledge that we shall always march ahead," still looms large for me today. Even more so, his call to "cash the check" of economic justice has inspired my work in business and philanthropy to provide pathways to education, STEM careers, and capital formation for African Americans.

What part of King's mission
resonates most with you?
How has persistence and
overcoming played a role
in your own march?

Dr. King with (left to right) activist Reverend Ralph Abernathy; his mother, Alberta Williams King; nurse Louise Stone; and civil rights leader Coretta Scott King, New York, September 30, 1958.

TPLP / Getty Images

The Beloved Community

"Justice Without Violence"

Thank you so much Dr. Himelhoch, to the president of this great university, members of the student body, ladies and gentlemen. I need to pause to say how happy I am to be here this evening, and to be a part of this lecture series. I have had a great deal of admiration for Brandeis University from its very beginning. From its liberalism and for its rich academic emphasis. I will always appreciate that, and I am sure that people all over this nation will be grateful, they are grateful now, and they will be in the future, for what Brandeis is doing for the cultural life of the nation.

I want to speak this evening about the race problem in a general sense, and more specifically about nonviolence. We hear a great deal about nonviolence when we speak of Montgomery, Alabama, and since I come from Montgomery, people expect me to say something about nonviolence from time to time. And so this evening we are using as a subject "Justice Without Violence."

It is impossible to look out into the broad arena of American life without noticing a real crisis in the area of race relations. This crisis has been precipitated on the one hand by the determined resistance of reactionary elements in the South to the Supreme Court's momentous decision outlawing segregation in the public schools, and as you well know, this resistance has often risen to ominous proportions. Many states have risen up in open defiance, and the legislative halls of the South ring loud with such words as *interposition*, and *nullification*. In many states the Ku Klux Klan is alive again; and also in many states we find the modern version of the Ku Klux Klan in the form of so-called respectable White Citizens' Councils. And all of these forces have conjoined to make for massive resistance.

The crisis has been precipitated on the other hand by the radical change in the Negro's evaluation of himself. It is probably true to say that there would be no crisis in race relations if the Negro thought of himself in inferior terms and patiently accepted injustice and exploitation that it is in this area, it is precisely here that the change has come. If we will but look at the history of the Negro in America we will see this change in terms that are crystal clear.

It was in the year of 1619 that the first slaves landed on the shores of this nation. They were brought here from the shores of Africa. Unlike the Pilgrim Fathers who landed at Plymouth a year later, they were brought here against their will. Throughout slavery, the Negro was treated in a very inhuman fashion. He was a thing to be used, not a person to be respected. He was merely a depersonalized cog in the vast plantation machine.

Certainly the famous Dred Scott decision of 1857 well illustrates the status of the Negro during slavery. It was within this decision that the Supreme Court of the nation said in substance that the Negro is not a citizen of this nation; he is merely property subject to the dictates of his owner. Even after his emancipation in 1863, the Negro still confronted oppression and inequality. It is true that for a period, while the army of occupation remained in the South, and Reconstruction ruled, the Negro enjoyed a period of eminence and political power, but he was soon overwhelmed by the white majority.

And pretty soon after that he experienced a new kind of slavery, covered up with certain niceties of complexity. And you will remember that in 1896 the Supreme Court came out with another decision, known as the *Plessy v. Ferguson* decision. In this decision the Supreme Court established the doctrine of separate beliefs and of the law of the land. And we all know the results of this oppressive doctrine. There was always a strict enforcement of the separate, without the slightest intention to abide by the equal. And so as a result the world kept the doctrine. The Negro ended up being plunged across the brink of exploitation, rather than experience the bleakness of nagging despair. Living under these conditions the Negroes lost faith in themselves. They came to feel that perhaps they were less than human, which is always the tragedy of physical slavery. It always ends up in the paralysis of mental slavery. And so long as the Negro accepted this place assigned to him, so long as he thought of himself in inferior terms, a sort of racial peace existed. But it was an uneasy peace, it was a negative peace. So you see true peace is not merely the absence of some negative force, it is the presence of justice. And the peace that existed at that time was a negative peace, an obnoxious peace, devoid of any positive meaning.

But then something happened to the Negro, and circumstances made it necessary for him to travel more. His rural plantation background was gradually being supplanted by migration to urban and industrial communities. His cultural life was gradually rising through the steady decline of crippling illiteracy. Even the economic life of the Negro was gradually rising to decisive proportions. And all of these factors came together to cause the Negro to take a new look at himself.

The Negro masses all over began to reevaluate themselves, and the Negro came to feel that he was somebody; his religion revealed to him that God loved all of his children, and that all are made in his image. And so he came to see and to feel in his own soul that the significant thing about a man is not his specificity but his fundamentals, and not the texture of his hair or the color of his skin, but the texture and quality of his soul.

And with this new evaluation, with this new self-respect, the negative peace of the nation and of the South was gradually undermined. The tension which we witness in the Southland today can be explained in part by the revolutionary change in the Negro's evaluation of his nature and destiny, and his determination to struggle and sacrifice and suffer until the sagging walls of segregation have finally been crushed by the battering rams of surging justice. This is the meaning of the crisis.

Now this determination on the part of American Negroes to free themselves from every form of discrimination and oppression stems from the same deep longing for human dignity, and for freedom expressed by oppressed people all over the world. The rhythmic beat of the deep rumblings, the discontent that we hear from Asia and Africa can be explained by the determination to break loose from the shackles of colonialism and imperialism, and stand up with dignity and with honor.

As we face this problem we must think of two basic facts. Whenever you have a struggle, sometimes it takes a long time to develop, and this struggle has taken a long time to develop certainly. It has been developing over the years. But let us remember this, that the struggle will continue. Why? On the one hand, history seems to prove and it seems to be sociologically true that privileged classes do not give up their privileges without strong resistance.

It also seems to be historically and sociologically true that once oppressed people rise up against that oppression, there is no stopping point short of full freedom. We must face the fact that the struggle will probably continue until freedom is a reality for the oppressed people of the world.

Now the question that we face this evening is this: In the light of the fact that the oppressed people of the world are rising up against that oppression; in the light of the fact that the American Negro is rising up against his oppression, the question is this: How will the struggle for justice be waged? And I think that is one of the most important questions confronting our generation. As we move to make justice a reality on the international scale, as we move to make justice a reality in this nation, how will the struggle be waged?

It seems to me that there are two possible answers to this question. One is to use the all-too-prevalent method of physical violence. And it is true that man throughout history has sought to achieve justice through violence. And we all know the danger of this method. It seems to create many more social problems than it solves. And it seems to me that in the struggle for justice, this method is ultimately futile.

If the Negro succumbs to the temptation of using violence in his struggle for justice, unborn generations will be the recipients of a long and desolate life of bitterness, and his chief legacy to the future will be an endless reign of meaningless chaos. And there is still a voice crying into the vista of time, saying to every potential Peter, "Put up your sword." And history is replete with the bleached bones of nations and communities that failed to follow this command.

So let us move from this method. This is one method, this is one way to seek justice through violence, but it seems to me that the weakness of this method is its futility. It creates many more problems than it solves.

But there is an alternative to violence. We may think of this alternative as a method of nonviolence, of nonviolent resistance, for you see it is possible to achieve justice through nonviolence. This method has been made famous in our generation by the work of Mohandas K. Gandhi, who lived in India not many years ago, and who used this method to free his people from the political domination, the economic exploitation and humiliation inflicted upon them by Britain. And he, I imagine, proved more than anybody else in the modern world that this can be an effective method, in seeking justice, in seeking to break loose from oppression.

Now let us look at this method and analyze it a bit and see what it says and see if it might not be used in the midst of the crisis which we confront in race relations in America, and the crisis which we confront all over the world with oppressed people rising up against their oppression.

The first thing that we can say about this method that seeks justice without violence is that it is not a method of cowardice or stagnant passivity; it's not a method to be used by persons filled with fear; by persons who are merely lacking in weapons of violence. It is not a method of cowardice. As Mohandas Gandhi used to say, "If the only alternative is that between violence and cowardice, I would say use violence," but it is good that there is another alternative.

And this is not a method of cowardice, and I also said that it is not a method of stagnant passivity. Sometimes the word *passive* misleads us because it gives the impression that this is a sort of sit-down do-nothing method. The sort of method that is nonactive. But nonviolence does not mean nonactivity. The nonviolent resister is just as opposed to the evil that he is protesting against, as the violent resister. This method does resist.

Now it is true that this method is passive in the sense that the nonviolent resister is not aggressive toward his opponent in a physical sense, with physical violence, but the mind and emotions are always active, and every moment seeking to convince and to persuade the opponent that he is wrong. This method is passive physically but strongly active spiritually. It is nonaggressive physically but dynamically aggressive spiritually.

There are certain things we can say about this method that seeks justice without violence. It does not seek to defeat or humiliate the opponent but to win his friendship and understanding. I think that this is one of the points, one of the basic points, one of the basic distinguishing points between violence and nonviolence. The ultimate end of violence is to defeat the opponent. The ultimate end of nonviolence is to win the friendship of the opponent.

It is necessary to boycott sometimes, but the nonviolent resister realizes that boycott is never an end within itself, but merely a means to awaken a sense of shame within the oppressor; that the end is reconciliation; the end is redemption. And so the aftermath of violence is bitterness; the aftermath of nonviolence is the creation of the Beloved Community; the aftermath of nonviolence is redemption and reconciliation. This is a method that seeks to transform and to redeem, and win the friendship of the opponent, and make it possible for men to live together as brothers in a community, and not continually live with bitterness and friction.

A third thing that we can say about this method is that it directs its attack at systems of evil rather than individuals who may be caught up in the system. In other words, this method seeks to defeat evil rather than individuals who may happen to be evil, who may happen to be victimized with evil. And this is the thing that we must see in race relations, it seems to me. As I like to say to the people in Montgomery—the tension in this city is not so much between Negro people and white people, but the tension is at bottom between justice and injustice; between the forces of life and the forces of darkness—and if that is the victory cry in Montgomery, it will not be a victory merely for the fifty thousand Negroes, but it will be a victory for justice; a victory for the forces of light; a victory for goodwill.

We must come to see that the festering sore of segregation debilitates the white man as well as the Negro. It gives the Negro a false sense of inferiority; it gives the white man a false sense of superiority, thereby distorting the personality of both. As we seek to remove the barrier of segregation, it must always be stressed that it is not sought merely to straighten out conditions for the Negro, but for all people; for all people involved in the system affected by it. We seek to defeat the evil system rather than individuals who happen to be caught up in the system. And I think that is a vital aspect of the method of nonviolence. Violence defeats individuals and so often fails to get back to the causal factor. The nonviolence goes beneath the surface and seeks to remove the cause or basis which is the evil system itself.

There is another basic thing about this method which seeks to achieve justice through nonviolence. It not only avoids external physical violence, but also internal violence of spirit. The nonviolent resister realizes that love should forever be at the forefront of his thinking. And as we struggle for justice as oppressed people all over the world struggle for justice and freedom and human dignity, it is my great hope that we will never succumb to the temptation of indulging in hate campaigns or becoming bitter. For if we hate for hate, if we try to solve the problem by hating in return, we do nothing but intensify the existence of hate in the universe, and somebody has to have some sense in this world and cut off the chain of hate. That is done through loving.

So this is a method that not only avoids external physical violence, but also internal violence to the spirit, which is hate and bitterness and malice. Oppressed people must continue to fight for justice passionately. Fight at all times with clean hands, always avoiding malice and hate; bitterness and falsehood.

Now I know you are looking at me and saying, somebody is saying that this is pretty difficult. To say, "Love your enemies," to love those people who seek to oppress you, to love those people who are trampling over you every day; that is almost impossible, some of you are probably saying. Well, I guess it is pretty difficult and it's pretty impossible and I guess it's almost absurd for me to say to anybody—"Love those who oppress you," in any affectionate and sentimental sense—and so when I speak of love here I am not talking about something affectionate and sentimental; I am talking about understanding goodwill for all men. A type of love that seeks to redeem.

It is very interesting, if you will notice, that the Greek language has three words for love. And it might give us a little clearance at this point.

The Greek language talks, for instance, about *Eros*. You know Plato talks about Eros in his dialogue. In Platonic philosophy this is a sort of yearning of the souls for the realm of the gods. For us it has come to be a sort of romantic love. For Plato it was an aesthetic love. For us it has come to be a sort of romantic love and it's vital. Eros is a vital type of love.

We read about beautiful Portia and it seems to express something of Eros. I guess that's what Shakespeare was talking about when he said, "Love is not love which alters when it alteration finds or bends with the remover to remove. O, no, it is an ever-fixèd mark that looks on tempests and is never shaken; it is the star to every wand'ring bark." You know I can remember that because I used to quote it to my wife when we were courting. That's Eros.

Then the Greek talks again about *Philia*, a sort of love, the type of love we have for personal friends; a sort of reciprocal love. And that is vital also. A love that loves because it is loved. On this level we love because we are loved. This is maybe the type of love that you have for your roommate, you see. A sort of, well, it is an affectionate type of love. And here you love because you are loved. The reciprocal love we have for personal friends.

But then the Greek language comes out and talks about *Agape*, and that is another interesting word. The New Testament places it as one of the highest forms of love. This is more than Eros, more than Philia; it's a redeeming type of love, it's a transforming type of love. The biblical theologians would say this is the love of God working in the lives of men. It is a love that seeks nothing in return; it loves everybody not because they are particularly likable but because God loves them. And it is at this point that I think love can be very vital.

And so we come to love all men, not because they're likable, not because we like the way they act. And it is interesting that there is a passage in the Bible which says "Love your enemies," and I am very happy it doesn't say, "Like your enemies." It's pretty difficult to like some people. Like is an affectionate sort of thing. You like to be with some people. You like their attitudes, you like the way they think, you like the way they act. That's an affectionate sort of thing, and you like them. But there are some people that it is pretty difficult to like. I find it rather difficult to like Senator Eastland. I find it difficult.

But there is an ethical something which says to me, "Love Senator Eastland," and love is greater than like. And this is what we seem to stress here when we talk about nonviolence on this level of the eternal side, where we cease not only to shoot a man but we cease to hate a man. It is a type of love that loves the individual who does the evil deed while hating the deed that the person does. And I think that when we rise to this level, nonviolence becomes quite meaningfully right.

There is a final thing that I want to say, and then I will leave it with you to ask questions. And there is a thing about this method that at least holds me together, and I have to stress it because I think it is very basic, at least it has been for my life. This method seems to stress the fact that the universe is on the side of justice. Sometimes it is very difficult to believe that. This is why the nonviolent resister can accept suffering without retaliating with violence, because he knows the universe is on the side of justice and it gives one a great faith in the future.

A nonviolent resister knows that in his struggle for justice, he is not alone, but that he has cosmic companionship, and that the moral laws of the universe somehow work together for the molding of justice and freedom and goodwill. Now I realize that there are those that believe in nonviolence who do not necessarily believe in a personal God. But I believe that even those persons, if they believe firmly in nonviolence, believe that at least there is something that moves toward justice in the universe.

It so happens that I have deep faith, an abiding faith in a personal God. Not some Aristotelian unmoved mover who merely contemplates upon himself. Not only a self-knowing God, but an ever-loving God who is concerned about the affairs of history. It is my conviction that God works through history for the salvation of man. And there is something in this universe that works for the molding of justice and goodwill and freedom.

There is something in this universe which justifies Carlyle in saying "no lie can live forever." There is something in this universe which justifies William Cullen Bryant in saying "truth forever on the scaffel, wrong forever on the throng, yet that scaffel sways a future; and behind dim unknown stands God within the shadow keeping watch above his own." And I am sure that is why down in Montgomery we can walk and never get weary, because we realize that there is a great camp meeting in the promised land of freedom and justice.

And so this is the method of nonviolent resistance. It seems to me that this is the method that can achieve justice, a method that can achieve it without violence, a method that can bring justice into being, and bring us to the point where we can all live together as brothers. It is my deep prayer that as we struggle together in Montgomery and all over the South, as people all over the world struggle for justice and freedom, they will struggle with this weapon of love and nonviolence.

It seems to me that if we will do this with dignity, with the proper attitude, and the proper discipline, we will be able to emerge from the bleak and desolate midnight of man's inhumanity to man, to the bright and glittering daybreak of freedom and justice. That will be the day when we can all cry, figuratively speaking, that a new day has come into being. And that will be the day, figuratively speaking, when the morning stars will sing together and the sons of God will shout for joy. Thank you.

—Dr. Martin Luther King Jr.

April 3, 1957, Brandeis University, Waltham, Massachusetts

Dr. King's vision of the Beloved Community was a society where people came together, supported one another, and worked collectively to move forward. This idea has always resonated with me—not just because of speeches like "Justice Without Violence," but because I saw it in action. My own community was a microcosm of that Beloved Community, showing me firsthand how the collective grew stronger when folks supported, protected, and enriched each other.

When I think of community, I naturally think about summers in northeast Denver, where I grew up. On balmy Friday afternoons, my neighbors would organize fish fries in backyards. Dozens of families convened on manicured lawns behind our homes, swapped stories, laughed, and bonded as they cradled plates of sizzling whitefish. On clear days, you could see the Rocky Mountains towering in the distance. When the sun started to go down, someone would bring out a slide projector, and one of the families would bring the slides they had created from their summer photo album. We would watch slideshows of summer trips to Alabama or Mississippi for hours under the starlight. Amid the blades of grass, all the kids played, drank soda pop, and ate popcorn.

As a Black American community in the 1970s, we were just beginning to embrace what Martin Luther King Jr. had fought and won for us: the hope and promise of integration into broader society. Still, the remnants of Jim Crow lingered, weakened but present. We were cautiously optimistic yet unsure of what was to come. The world around us was changing for the better, but old prejudices remained. And while things were getting better, there still was a long way to go for us to gain full acceptance. However, during our gatherings on midsummer evenings, you would never have known how unsettled the outside world was for us. We held a space for each other that was loving, safe, and joyful.

We existed in a "Beloved Community," a concept dear to Dr. King's heart and carried forward by his daughter Bernice, who lives today in Atlanta. For Dr. King, a Beloved Community was a harmonious society where individuals collaborated, enhanced each other's lives, and cultivated a more benevolent world. Fortunately for me, this vision was not an abstract ideal—it was a palpable reality, deeply impactful during my youth. Dr. King said, "Our objective is to cultivate a Beloved Community, a task that necessitates quantitative improvements in our material circumstances but a profound qualitative transformation within our very souls."

My neighborhood in northeast Denver where I spent my formative years in the 1960s and 1970s was an enclave between Five Points and Lincoln Hills. It was a neighborhood of tree-lined streets with modest ranch-style homes peppered with the occasional Victorian-style houses, populated by dentists, teachers, elected leaders, Pullman porters, contractors, small business owners, and pharmacists. We were an ambitious and hardworking bunch who took pride in helping each other. Most of our families had made their way over generations during the Great Migration, taking root in a city a mile high in the sky.

My family's roots stretched back to Tennessee, Texas, and Oklahoma. Some of my clan lived in Tulsa in an area popularly known as Black Wall Street. Part of the clan were ministers and teachers. My paternal grandmother's side of the family, the Vaden and the Ramsay clans, owned a pool hall and hardware store in Tulsa. They were part of a brief dream of economic opportunity for Black Americans at the turn of the century before their Beloved Community was massacred and the survivors expelled from Greenwood, Tulsa, in 1921. Greenwood emerged in Tulsa during the oil boom at the turn of the century and became Black America's shining city on a hill. Its vibrant business district fostered a strong Black middle class and entrepreneurial spirit, while its outstanding schools offered enrichment and opportunity for its youth. It stood as a paragon of what Black Americans could achieve when given the chance. Tragically, it was this ideal—that Black excellence could thrive—that led to the violent destruction of Greenwood during the Tulsa Race Massacre of 1921. The community was burned to the ground and firebombed by those who could not bear to see such progress. In an instant, the dream of a Beloved Community was shattered.

In January 2025, the Justice Department issued a report on the massacre, shedding new light on this horrific event. Assistant Attorney General Kristen Clarke described the massacre as "unique in its magnitude, barbarity, and racist hostility," and emphasized that it was not simply a riot or mob violence but a "coordinated, military-style attack." The assault on Greenwood left many homes and businesses destroyed, firebombed, and scorched, obliterating entire blocks. To add insult to injury, survivors were left with little recourse or support, as the City of Tulsa resisted meaningful aid, and attempts to seek restitution through the justice system were thwarted. According to the Justice Department report, those who tried to rebuild faced harsh obstacles, including new, prohibitively expensive fire codes imposed by the city.

In Denver, our community had been cordoned off by redlining and racism, segregated from the white side of town. But the forced proximity knit our families together, and from those bonds of shared struggle and culture grew a nurturing desire to watch out for each other and to make life better.

We were known for Five Points, a business district in Denver with several renowned clubs and theaters that attracted some of the best Black entertainers. It was known as the "Harlem of the West." I remember stories of folks like Duke Ellington, Count Basie, and Sarah Vaughn coming to Five Points to perform and visit with families in my neighborhood. During the Jim Crow era, Black entertainers could not lodge at hotels in Denver where white patrons stayed. Instead, they lodged in the Rossonian Hotel in our downtown, which was listed in *The Negro Motorist Green Book*, or in Lincoln Hills, a vacation resort for Black people.

Lincoln Hills was a special place. Folks in my community spent summers in cabins at the resort of rolling green hills and pine forests. It was one of the few vacation resorts for Black people, the only one west of the Mississippi. My dad spent most of his summertime there studying and fishing. My first visit was in a bassinet when I was six months old. As an adult, I've been investing in Lincoln Hills to grow it as a summer retreat for more young people and increase prosperity for more people in Five Points.

In our community, we all tried to bring something positive to each other's lives. On the Fourth of July some adults put on a fireworks show for the kids. On Memorial Day, the men who had served would don their medals and military regalia. It was a cherished tradition to see the different generations in their neatly pressed full-dress uniforms from their respective service tours in World War I, World War II, the Korean War, and Vietnam. Some of the men, like my father and uncle, were commissioned officers—lieutenant and major, respectively—a rarity for African Americans at the time. They were part of a proud tradition of service in the African American community. During World Wars I and II, Black men made up about 10 percent of enlistees. In the Korean War, African Americans accounted for approximately 13 percent of the US military and about 12 percent of those who died in combat. In the Vietnam War, despite making up just 12.6 percent of the US population, African Americans accounted for nearly 20 percent of combat deaths.

The business owners and professionals who operated our storefronts and taught in our schools were proud to serve the Black community, and our parents worked hard to provide a safe and nurturing environment for kids in our neighborhood. They all put together a debutante ball for the girls at a place called the Owl Club. One year I served as an escort and donned full formal attire. It was fun for us to get dressed up and for our parents to come together and display their pride. I think back now and realize how much effort the adults made to ensure my peers and I felt loved and valued.

Life felt surprisingly fair as a boy, even though the world was anything but fair for Black people. It felt that way because the adults shielded us from injustice. They knew what awaited us and created a loving cocoon where we could grow. To be sure, they faced indignity, discrimination, and sometimes violence. In the hallways of our homes, we would overhear someone whisper about being passed over for a job or promotion or getting paid less because of the color of their skin. But for the most part, they absorbed the arrows with strength and fortitude so that we could grow and develop the skills and mindset needed to succeed as adults. They wanted to keep us optimistic and make us believe that America was better than it actually was.

Since most of the parents in my community worked, kids in my neighborhood usually walked to Mrs. Brown's home after school. She was a tall, well-put-together woman with beautiful brown skin and a broad, warm, welcoming smile. Mrs. Brown's home was more than just an informal after-school program; it was a place where we were nurtured. Mrs. Brown was incredible. She kept us safe, fed us nutritious snacks, and ensured we did our homework (the right way). She taught us about responsibility and looking out for one another. She did more than look after us; she enriched our lives as children. Because her house was filled with kids of all ages, I had older boys and girls all around me who served as role models. They studied hard and believed in themselves. They would take time to tutor us younger kids. Mrs. Brown also ensured we all got home safely and walked us home if our parents had to work late.

Many other neighbors played similarly supportive roles. Our local priest visited with families in our enclave. I fondly recall Father Thaddeus Posey coming over for dinner every Sunday, and enjoying a whiskey with my father after dinner. Another neighbor, Mr. Denny, was intelligent and friendly, with a kind face and curly hair. He was into science and showed a group of kids in my neighborhood how to build rockets. Many of us who made rockets with Mr. Denny ended up in careers in science and technology. His small investment of time in a bunch of neighborhood kids paid immeasurable dividends. Expanding access to this type of enrichment, particularly for African American children, is one of many ways we can build Beloved Communities for more young people today.

Young people need to participate in the growing tech economy, and providing enrichment and mentorship through after-school coding, math, and STEM programs is essential for fulfilling educational needs beyond the classroom. It's an effective way to spark interest in STEM fields, much as my neighbor, Mr. Homer Denny, did for us. For example, there's an after-school program called SEO in New York that I'm a big fan of. However, it's only available to less than 0.01 percent of the students of color. But the kids in SEO get fifteen extra hours of education a week. Not surprisingly, more than 99 percent of their students go to college. SEO is a model of what is possible if we implement more academic after-school programs focused on STEM.

In my childhood community, it wasn't just the kids who had each other's backs; the adults supported each other too. I remember the party in our backyard when my dad earned his doctorate in 1972. Our yard overflowed with friends and neighbors wishing us well and congratulating my dad. It felt as if the whole neighborhood celebrated alongside him, as though everyone had received that doctorate. Days later, people kept coming by and knocking on our door to shake my dad's hand.

In 1974, when I was around twelve, Mrs. Brown's husband, George Brown, decided to run for lieutenant governor of Colorado. Mr. Brown was a state senator and former Tuskegee Airman, beloved in our neighborhood. He had a salt-and-pepper mustache, a closely cropped Afro, thick glasses, a friendly demeanor, and a big smile. We knew he cared about our interests, so we supported him. We wore out our shoe leather, knocking on doors and canvassing for our neighbors. When all the votes were tallied, Mr. Brown was declared the winner. He became the first Black lieutenant governor of Colorado. We shocked the Centennial State. Our belief in each other and what we could do together was affirmed. To celebrate this momentous win, we had a cookout in the Browns' backyard, where Mrs. Brown always took care of us neighborhood kids. We rejoiced and feasted together on her home cooking in the glade underneath the wide-open Colorado sky. We felt like David slaying Goliath that evening. At the time, Black Americans were only 3 percent of the Colorado population. Today, we make up nearly 5 percent.

The first significant snow after Lieutenant Governor Brown was elected allowed us to test our political muscle. In March 1975, a few months after Mr. Brown was sworn in, we got a few feet of snow. After the blizzard, schools were closed for two or three days, and children remained stuck home with their parents. Eventually, a snowplow came and plowed one stripe down the middle of our street. Families had to dig their own cars out just to get to work. When we would venture out to the white side of town a few miles away after a big snow, it was a different story. The streets were cleared quickly after the snow stopped. It was a stark contrast.

Through our community civic association, my father and Lieutenant Governor Brown eventually hammered out a deal with the city to clear our streets so Black folks could get to their jobs. It may sound like a small thing, but if people couldn't get to work during snow days, they wouldn't get paid, so ensuring the streets were plowed protected people's jobs and income. This was the Beloved Community in action.

Martin Luther King Jr. was born in the African American enclave of Sweet Auburn, Atlanta, a Beloved Community in its own right. He spoke about how his community, composed of working-class and middle-class Black folk, was safe, loving, and neighborly. His mother, Alberta Williams King, nurtured self-respect in her children. She tutored them and taught them how to play the piano. She instilled in them a sense of "somebodiness," as King put it. His father, Martin Luther King Sr., was a loving patriarch and husband, a pastor in the activist Black prophetic tradition, and the president of the Atlanta NAACP. Young Martin's formative years were spent around his father's organizing for civil rights. As a teenager, he attended Booker T. Washington High School, the first high school established for Black youth in Atlanta. His predominantly Black teachers and administrators recognized his intellectual gifts. They pushed him to graduate early and matriculate at age fifteen to the historically Black

Morehouse College (another Beloved Community), steering him toward his world-changing path.

The importance of a Beloved Community cannot be overstated. The villages that raised Dr. King and me gave us the confidence, resources, and support to grow into our adult selves. Even when the broader world was hostile, our villages were there to nurture and help us thrive. John Lewis, an ally of Dr. King's, once said, "Each of us must do our part to help build the Beloved Community." This can be distilled into support, enrichment, and protection. We can all work toward creating a safe, warm, secure, and harmonious environment within our local communities. We also can work to facilitate academic enrichment for kids outside the classroom. This can take several forms, from creating a safe space similar to Mrs. Brown's to being a mentor like Mr. Denny and making great after-school STEM programs.

Community-level organizing is equally indispensable. In the same breath, John Lewis also said, "When you see something that is not right, you must say something. You must do something." My community rallied together to elect George Brown and convince the city to ensure our streets were plowed so that our people could get to work. In the same way, this unity can manifest today if individuals mobilize, organize, and elevate leaders who prioritize the greater good of their neighbors and community members, especially on issues like education, economic opportunity, and fundamental rights. This is the bedrock upon which we can build more Beloved Communities today.

Growing up in a Beloved Community taught me a vital lesson: When people support, protect, and enrich each other's lives, the collective grows stronger than its individual parts. Dr. King talked about looking after one's fellow man, or *agape*, and endeavoring to build Beloved Communities. These concepts provided a model of centering cooperation and service in my business, philanthropy, and leadership work. My experiences have taught me that incredible things can happen when people collaborate to reach a greater goal.

What role should you play in creating Beloved Communities, where members protect each other and enrich each other's lives while beautifying their neighborhoods? Consider how you can contribute to fostering unity, support, and positive change within your community.

Dr. King speaks at a rally in Chicago, July 24, 1965.

Bettmann

The Two Americas

"The Other America"

Mr. Bell, members of the faculty and members of the student body of this great institution of learning; ladies and gentlemen.

Now there are several things that one could talk about before such a large, concerned, and enlightened audience. There are so many problems facing our nation and our world, that one could just take off anywhere. But today I would like to talk mainly about the race problems since I'll have to rush right out and go to New York to talk about Vietnam tomorrow. And I've been talking about it a great deal this week and weeks before that.

But I'd like to use a subject from which to speak this afternoon, the Other America.

And I use this subject because there are literally two Americas. One America is beautiful for situation. And, in a sense, this America is overflowing with the milk of prosperity and the honey of opportunity. This America is the habitat of millions of people who have food and material necessities for their bodies; and culture and education for their minds; and freedom and human dignity for their spirits. In this America, millions of people experience every day the opportunity of having life, liberty, and the pursuit of happiness in all of their dimensions. And in this America millions of young people grow up in the sunlight of opportunity.

But tragically and unfortunately, there is another America. This Other America has a daily ugliness about it that constantly transforms the ebulliency of hope into the fatigue of despair. In this America millions of work-starved men walk the streets daily in search for jobs that do not exist. In this America millions of people find themselves living in rat-infested, vermin-filled slums. In this America people are poor by the millions. They find themselves perishing on a lonely island of poverty in the midst of a vast ocean of material prosperity.

In a sense, the greatest tragedy of this other America is what it does to little children. Little children in this other America are forced to grow up with clouds of inferiority forming every day in their little mental skies. As we look at this other America, we see it as an arena of blasted hopes and shattered dreams. Many people of various backgrounds live in this other America. Some are Mexican Americans, some are Puerto Ricans, some are Indians, some happen to be from other groups. Millions of them are Appalachian whites. But probably the largest group in this other America in proportion to its size in the population is the American Negro.

The American Negro finds himself living in a triple ghetto. A ghetto of race, a ghetto of poverty, a ghetto of human misery. So what we are seeking to do in the civil rights movement is to deal with this problem. To deal with this problem of the two Americas. We are seeking to make America one nation, indivisible, with liberty and justice for all. Now let me say that the struggle for civil rights and the struggle to make these two Americas one America is much more difficult today than it was five or ten years ago. For about a decade or maybe twelve years, we've struggled all across the South in glorious struggles to get rid of legal, overt segregation and all of the humiliation that surrounded that system of segregation.

In a sense this was a struggle for decency; we could not go to a lunch counter in so many instances and get a hamburger or a cup of coffee. We could not make use of public accommodations. Public transportation was segregated, and often we had to sit in the back and within transportation—transportation within cities—we often had to stand over empty seats because sections were reserved for whites only. We did not have the right to vote in so many areas of the South. And the struggle was to deal with these problems.

And certainly they were difficult problems, they were humiliating conditions. By the thousands we protested these conditions. We made it clear that it was ultimately more honorable to accept jail cell experiences than to accept segregation and humiliation. By the thousands, students and adults decided to sit in at segregated lunch counters to protest conditions there. When they were sitting at those lunch counters they were in reality standing up for the best in the American dream and seeking to take the whole nation back to those great wells of democracy which were dug deep by the Founding Fathers in the formulation of the Constitution and the Declaration of Independence.

Many things were gained as a result of these years of struggle. In 1964 the civil rights bill came into being after the Birmingham movement, which did a great deal to subpoena the conscience of a large segment of the nation to appear before the judgment seat of morality on the whole question of civil rights. After the Selma movement in 1965 we were able to get a voting rights bill. And all of these things represented strides.

But we must see that the struggle today is much more difficult. It's more difficult today because we are struggling now for genuine equality. It's much easier to integrate a lunch counter than it is to guarantee a livable income and a good solid job. It's much easier to guarantee the right to vote than it is to guarantee the right to live in sanitary, decent housing conditions. It is much easier to integrate a public park than it is to make genuine, quality, integrated education a reality. And so today we are struggling for something which says we demand genuine equality.

It's not merely a struggle against extremist behavior toward Negroes. And I'm convinced that many of the very people who supported us in the struggle in the South are not willing to go all the way now. I came to see this in a very difficult and painful way. In Chicago the last year where I've lived and worked. Some of the people who came quickly to march with us in Selma and Birmingham weren't active around Chicago. And I came to see that so many people who supported morally and even financially what we were doing in Birmingham and Selma were really outraged against the extremist behavior of Bull Connor and Jim Clark toward Negroes, rather than believing in genuine equality for Negroes. And I think this is what we've gotta see now, and this is what makes the struggle much more difficult.

So as a result of all of this, we see many problems existing today that are growing more difficult. It's something that is often overlooked, but Negroes generally live in worse slums today than twenty or twenty-five years ago. In the North, schools are more segregated today than they were in 1954 when the Supreme Court's decision on desegregation was rendered. Economically the Negro is worse off today than he was fifteen and twenty years ago. And so the unemployment rate among whites at one time was about the same as the unemployment rate among Negroes. But today the unemployment rate among Negroes is twice that of whites. And the average income of the Negro is today 50 percent less than whites.

As we look at these problems we see them growing and developing every day. We see the fact that the Negro economically is facing a depression in his everyday life that is more staggering than the depression of the thirties. The unemployment rate of the nation as a whole is about 4 percent. Statistics would say from the Labor Department that among Negroes it's about 8.4 percent. But these are the persons who are in the labor market, who still go to employment agencies to seek jobs, and so they can be calculated. The statistics can be gotten because they are still somehow in the labor market.

But there are hundreds of thousands of Negroes who have given up. They've lost hope. They've come to feel that life is a long and desolate corridor for them with no Exit sign, and so they no longer go to look for a job. There are those who would estimate that these persons, who are called the Discouraged Persons, these 6 or 7 percent in the Negro community, that means that unemployment among Negroes may well be 16 percent. Among Negro youth in some of our larger urban areas it goes to 30 and 40 percent. So you can see what I mean when I say that, in the Negro community, there is a major, tragic, and staggering depression that we face in our everyday lives.

Now the other thing that we've gotta come to see now that many of us didn't see too well during the last ten years—that is that racism is still alive in American society. And much more widespread than we realized. And we must see racism for what it is. It is a myth of the superior and the inferior race. It is the false and tragic notion that one particular group, one particular race is responsible for all of the progress, all of the insights in the total flow of history. And the theory that another group or another race is totally depraved, innately impure, and innately inferior.

In the final analysis, racism is evil because its ultimate logic is genocide. Hitler was a sick and tragic man who carried racism to its logical conclusion. He ended up leading a nation to the point of killing about 6 million Jews. This is the tragedy of racism, because its ultimate logic is genocide. If one says that I am not good enough to live next door to him; if one says that I am not good enough to eat at a lunch counter, or to have a good, decent job, or to go to school with him merely because of my race, he is saying consciously or unconsciously that I do not deserve to exist.

To use a philosophical analogy here, racism is not based on some empirical generalization; it is based rather on an ontological affirmation. It is not the assertion that certain people are behind culturally or otherwise because of environmental conditions. It is the affirmation that the very being of a people is inferior. And this is the great tragedy of it.

I submit that however unpleasant it is we must honestly see and admit that racism is still deeply rooted all over America. It is still deeply rooted in the North, and it's still deeply rooted in the South.

And this leads me to say something about another discussion that we hear a great deal, and that is the so-called "white backlash." I would like to honestly say to you that the white backlash is merely a new name for an old phenomenon. It's not something that just came into being because of shouts of "Black power," or because Negroes engaged in riots in Watts, for instance. The fact is that the state of California voted a fair housing bill out of existence before anybody shouted "Black power," or before anybody rioted in Watts.

It may well be that shouts of "Black power" and riots in Watts and the Harlems and the other areas are the consequences of the white backlash rather than the cause of them. What it is necessary to see is that there has never been a single, solid, monistic, determined commitment on the part of the vast majority of white Americans on the whole question of civil rights and on the whole question of racial equality. This is something that truth impels all men of goodwill to admit.

It is said on the Statue of Liberty that America is a home of exiles. It doesn't take us long to realize that America has been the home of its white exiles from Europe. But it has not evinced the same kind of maternal care and concern for its Black exiles from Africa. It is no wonder that in one of his sorrow songs, the Negro could sing out, "Sometimes I feel like a motherless child." What great estrangement, what great sense of rejection caused a people to emerge with such a metaphor as they looked over their lives.

What I'm trying to get across is that our nation has constantly taken a positive step forward on the question of racial justice and racial equality. But over and over again at the same time, it made certain backward steps. And this has been the persistence of the so-called white backlash.

In 1863 the Negro was freed from the bondage of physical slavery. But at the same time, the nation refused to give him land to make that freedom meaningful. And at that same period, America was giving millions of acres of land in the West and the Midwest, which meant that America was willing to undergird its white peasants from Europe with an economic floor that would make it possible to grow and develop, and refused to give that economic floor to its Black peasants, so to speak.

This is why Frederick Douglass could say that emancipation for the Negro was freedom to hunger, freedom to the winds and rains of heaven, freedom without roofs to cover their heads. He went on to say that it was freedom without bread to eat, freedom without land to cultivate. It was freedom and famine at the same time. But it does not stop there.

In 1875 the nation passed a civil rights bill and refused to enforce it. In 1964 the nation passed a weaker civil rights bill and even to this day, that bill has not been totally enforced in all of its dimensions. The nation heralded a new day of concern for the poor, for the poverty stricken, for the disadvantaged. And brought into being a poverty bill and at the same time it put such little money into the program that it was hardly, and still remains hardly, a good skirmish against poverty. White politicians in suburbs talk eloquently against open housing, and in the same breath contend that they are not racist. And all of this, and all of these things tell us that America has been backlashing on the whole question of basic constitutional and God-given rights for Negroes and other disadvantaged groups for more than three hundred years.

So these conditions, existence of widespread poverty, slums, and of tragic conniptions in schools and other areas of life, all of these things have brought about a great deal of despair, and a great deal of desperation. A great deal of disappointment and even bitterness in the Negro communities. And today all of our cities confront huge problems. All of our cities are potentially powder kegs as a result of the continued existence of these conditions. Many in moments of anger, many in moments of deep bitterness, engage in riots.

Let me say as I've always said, and I will always continue to say, that riots are socially destructive and self-defeating. I'm still convinced that nonviolence is the most potent weapon available to oppressed people in their struggle for freedom and justice. I feel that violence will only create more social problems than they will solve. That in a real sense it is impracticable for the Negro to even think of mounting a violent revolution in the United States. So I will continue to condemn riots, and continue to say to my brothers and sisters that this is not the way. And continue to affirm that there is another way.

But at the same time, it is as necessary for me to be as vigorous in condemning the conditions which cause persons to feel that they must engage in riotous activities as it is for me to condemn riots. I think America must see that riots do not develop out of thin air. Certain conditions continue to exist in our society which must be condemned as vigorously as we condemn riots. But in the final analysis, a riot is the language of the unheard. And what is it that America has failed to hear? It has failed to hear that the plight of the Negro poor has worsened over the last few years. It has failed to hear that the promises of freedom and justice have not been met. And it has failed to hear that large segments of white society are more concerned about tranquility and the status quo than about justice, equality, and humanity. And so in a real sense our nation's summers of riots are caused by our nation's winters of delay. And as long as America postpones justice, we stand in the position of having these recurrences of violence and riots over and over again. Social justice and progress are the absolute guarantors of riot prevention.

Now let me go on to say that if we are to deal with all of the problems that I've talked about, and if we are to bring America to the point that we have one nation, indivisible, with liberty and justice for all, there are certain things that we must do. The job ahead must be massive and positive. We must develop massive action programs all over the United States of America in order to deal with the problems that I have mentioned. Now in order to develop these massive action programs we've got to get rid of one or two false notions that continue to exist in our society. One is the notion that only time can solve the problem of racial injustice. I'm sure you've heard this idea. It is the notion almost that there is something in the very flow of time that will miraculously cure all evils. And I've heard this over and over again. There are those, and they are often sincere people, who say to Negroes and their allies in the white community that we should slow up and just be nice and patient and continue to pray, and in a hundred or two hundred years the problem will work itself out because only time can solve the problem.

I think there is an answer to that myth. And it is that time is neutral. It can be used either constructively or destructively. And I'm absolutely convinced that the forces of ill will in our nation, the extreme rightists in our nation, have often used time much more effectively than the forces of goodwill. And it may well be that we will have to repent in this generation not merely for the vitriolic words of the bad people and the violent actions of the bad people, but for the appalling silence and indifference of the good people who sit around and say, "Wait on time."

Somewhere we must come to see that social progress never rolls in on the wheels of inevitability. It comes through the tireless efforts and the persistent work of dedicated individuals. And without this hard work, time itself becomes an ally of the primitive forces of social stagnation. And so we must help time, and we must realize that the time is always right to do right.

Now there's another notion that gets out, it's around everywhere. It's in the South, it's in the North, it's in California, and all over our nation. It's the notion that legislation can't solve the problem, it can't do anything in this area. And those who project this argument contend that you've got to change the heart and that you can't change the heart through legislation. Now I would be the first one to say that there is real need for a lot of heart changing in our country, and I believe in changing the heart. I preach about it. I believe in the need for conversion in many instances, and regeneration, to use theological terms. And I would be the first to say that if the race problem in America is to be solved, the white person must treat the Negro right, not merely because the law says it, but because it's natural, because it's right, and because the Negro is his brother. And so I realize that if we are to have a truly integrated society, men and women will have to rise to the majestic heights of being obedient to the unenforceable.

But after saying this, let me say another thing which gives the other side, and that is that although it may be true that morality cannot be legislated, behavior can be regulated. Even though it may be true that the law cannot change the heart, it can restrain the heartless. Even though it may be true that the law cannot make a man love me, it can restrain him from lynching me. And I think that's pretty important also. And so while the law may not change the hearts of men, it can and it does change the habits of men. And when you begin to change the habits of men, pretty soon the attitudes will be changed; pretty soon the hearts will be changed. And I'm convinced that we still need strong civil rights legislation. And there is a bill before Congress right now to have a national or federal open housing bill. A federal law declaring discrimination in housing unconstitutional.

And also a bill to make the administration of justice real all over our country. Now nobody can doubt the need for this. Nobody can doubt the need if he thinks about the fact that since 1963 some fifty Negroes and white civil rights workers have been brutally murdered in the state of Mississippi alone, and not a single person has been convicted for these dastardly crimes. There have been some indictments but no one has been convicted. And so there is a need for a federal law dealing with the whole question of the administration of justice.

There is a need for fair housing laws all over our country. And it is tragic indeed that Congress last year allowed this bill to die. And when that bill died in Congress, a bit of democracy died, a bit of our commitment to justice died. If it happens again in this session of Congress, a greater degree of our commitment to democratic principles will die. And I can see no more dangerous trend in our country than the constant developing of predominantly Negro central cities ringed by white suburbs. This is only inviting social disaster. And the only way this problem will be solved is by the nation taking a strong stand, and by state governments taking a strong stand against housing segregation and against discrimination in all of these areas.

Now there's another thing that I'd like to mention as I talk about the massive action program, and time will not permit me to go into specific programmatic action to any great degree. But it must be realized now that the Negro cannot solve the problems by himself. There again, there are those who always say to Negroes, "Why don't you do something for yourself? Why don't you lift yourselves by your own bootstraps?" And we hear this over and over again.

Now certainly there are many things that we must do for ourselves, and that only we can do for ourselves. Certainly we must develop within a sense of dignity and self-respect that nobody else can give us. A sense of manhood, a sense of personhood, a sense of not being ashamed of our heritage, not being ashamed of our color. It was wrong and tragic of the Negro ever to allow himself to be ashamed of the fact that he was Black, or ashamed of the fact that his ancestral home was Africa. And so there is a great deal that the Negro can do to develop self-respect. There is a great deal that the Negro must do and can do to amass political and economic power within his own community and by using his own resources. And so we must do certain things for ourselves but this must not negate the fact, and cause the nation to overlook the fact, that the Negro cannot solve the problem himself.

A man was on the plane with me some weeks ago and he came up to me and said, "The problem, Dr. King, that I see with what you all are doing is that every time I see you and other Negroes, you're protesting and you aren't doing anything for yourselves." And he went on to tell me that he was very poor at one time, and he was able to make by doing something for himself. "Why don't you teach your people," he said, "to lift themselves by their own bootstraps?" And then he went on to say other groups faced disadvantages, the Irish, the Italian, and he went down the line.

And I said to him that it does not help the Negro, it only deepens his frustration, upon feeling insensitive people to say to him that other ethnic groups who migrated or were immigrants to this country less than a hundred years or so ago have gotten beyond him and he came here some 344 years ago. And I went on to remind him that the Negro came to this country involuntarily in chains, while others came voluntarily. I went on to remind him that no other racial group has been a slave on American soil. I went on to remind him that the other problem we have faced over the years is that this society placed a stigma on the color of the Negro, on the color of his skin because he was Black. Doors were closed to him that were not closed to other groups.

And I finally said to him that it's a nice thing to say to people that you oughta lift yourself by your own bootstraps, but it is a cruel jest to say to a bootless man that he oughta lift himself by his own bootstraps. And the fact is that millions of Negroes, as a result of centuries of denial and neglect, have been left bootless. They find themselves impoverished aliens in this affluent society. And there is a great deal that the society can and must do if the Negro is to gain the economic security that he needs.

Now one of the answers, it seems to me, is a guaranteed annual income, a guaranteed minimum income for all people, and for our families of our country. It seems to me that the civil rights movement must now begin to organize for the guaranteed annual income. Begin to organize people all over our country, and mobilize forces so that we can bring to the attention of our nation this need, and this is something which I believe will go a long, long way toward dealing with the Negro's economic problem and the economic problem which many other poor people confront in our nation. Now I said I wasn't going to talk about Vietnam, but I can't make a speech without mentioning some of the problems that we face there, because I think this war has diverted attention from civil rights. It has strengthened the forces of reaction in our country and has brought to the forefront the military-industrial complex that even President Eisenhower warned us against at one time. And above all, it is destroying human lives. It's destroying the lives of thousands of the young, promising men of our nation. It's destroying the lives of little boys and little girls in Vietnam.

But one of the greatest things that this war is doing to us in civil rights is that it is allowing the Great Society to be shot down on the battlefields of Vietnam every day. And I submit this afternoon that we can end poverty in the United States. Our nation has the resources to do it. The gross national product of America will rise to the astounding figure of some $780 billion this year. We have the resources: The question is whether our nation has the will, and I submit that if we can spend $35 billion a year to fight an ill-considered war in Vietnam, and $20 billion to put a man on the moon, our nation can spend billions of dollars to put God's children on their own two feet right here on earth.

Let me say another thing that's more in the realm of the spirit, I guess, that is that if we are to go on in the days ahead and make true brotherhood a reality, it is necessary for us to realize more than ever before that the destinies of the Negro and the white man are tied together. Now there are still a lot of people who don't realize this. The racists still don't realize this. But it is a fact now that Negroes and whites are tied together, and we need each other. The Negro needs the white man to save him from his fear. The white man needs the Negro to save him from his guilt. We are tied together in so many ways, our language, our music, our cultural patterns, our material prosperity, and even our food are an amalgam of black and white.

So there can be no separate Black path to power and fulfillment that does not intersect white groups. There can be no separate white path to power and fulfillment short of social disaster. It does not recognize the need of sharing that power with Black aspirations for freedom and justice. We must come to see now that integration is not merely a romantic or aesthetic something where you merely add color to a still predominantly white power structure. Integration must be seen also in political terms where there is shared power, where Black men and white men share power together to build a new and a great nation.

In a real sense, we are all caught in an inescapable network of mutuality, tied in a single garment of destiny. John Donne placed it years ago in graphic terms, "No man is an island entire of itself. Every man is a piece of the continent, a part of the main." And he goes on toward the end to say, "Any man's death diminishes me because I'm involved in mankind. Therefore, never send to know for whom the bell tolls. It tolls for thee." And so we are all in the same situation: The salvation of the Negro will mean the salvation of the white man. And the destruction of life and of the ongoing progress of the Negro will be the destruction of the ongoing progress of the nation.

Now let me say finally that we have difficulties ahead but I haven't despaired. Somehow, I maintain hope in spite of hope. And I've talked about the difficulties and how hard the problems will be as we tackle them. But I want to close by saying this afternoon that I still have faith in the future. And I still believe that these problems can be solved. And so I will not join anyone who will say that we still can't develop a coalition of conscience.

I realize and understand the discontent and the agony and the disappointment and even the bitterness of those who feel that whites in America cannot be trusted. And I would be the first to say that there are all too many who are still guided by the racist ethos. And I am still convinced that there are still many white persons of goodwill. And I'm happy to say that I see them every day in the student generation who cherish democratic principles and justice above principle, and who will stick with the cause of justice and the cause of civil rights and the cause of peace throughout the days ahead. And so I refuse to despair. I think we're gonna achieve our freedom because however much America strays away from the ideals of justice, the goal of America is freedom.

Abused and scorned though we may be, our destiny is tied up in the destiny of America. Before the Pilgrim Fathers landed at Plymouth, we were here. Before Jefferson etched across the pages of history the majestic words of the Declaration of Independence, we were here. Before the beautiful words of "The Star-Spangled Banner" were written, we were here. For more than two centuries, our forebearers labored here without wages. They made cotton king. They built the homes of their masters in the midst of the most humiliating and oppressive conditions. And yet out of a bottomless vitality, they continued to grow and develop.

And I say that if the inexpressible cruelties of slavery couldn't stop us, the opposition that we now face, including the so-called white backlash, will surely fail. We're gonna win our freedom because both the sacred heritage of our nation and the eternal will of the Almighty God are embodied in our echoing demands.

And so I can still sing "We Shall Overcome." We shall overcome because the arc of the moral universe is long but it bends toward justice. We shall overcome because Carlyle is right, "No lie can live forever." We shall overcome because William Cullen Bryant is right, "Truth crushed to earth will rise again." We shall overcome because James Russell Lowell is right, "Truth forever on the scaffold, Wrong forever on the throne—yet that scaffold sways the future." With this faith, we will be able to hew out of the mountain of despair a stone of hope.

With this faith, we will be able to transform the jangling discourse of our nation into a beautiful symphony of brotherhood. With this faith, we will be able to speed up the day when all of God's children, Black men and white men, Jews and Gentiles, Protestants and Catholics, will be able to join hands and live together as brothers and sisters, all over this great nation. That will be a great day, that will be a great tomorrow. In the words of the Scripture, to speak symbolically, that will be the day when the morning stars will sing together and the sons of God will shout for joy.

—Dr. Martin Luther King Jr.

April 14, 1967, Stanford University, Stanford, California

In "The Other America," Dr. King exposed the divide between privilege and poverty. He emphasized that true equality demands economic justice. His words remind us that civil rights alone aren't enough. We must create pathways to opportunity through education, fair wages, and community investment. This vision drives my work to help close these gaps and provide opportunity for those who have been left behind.

In 1970, two years after the Civil Rights Act was signed into law, Denver inaugurated a busing program to desegregate its schools. Students from my neighborhood were slated to be transported to Carson Elementary, a high-performing school five miles east in the tree-lined highlands. Families in my community couldn't help but feel optimistic about their children's educational prospects. Their hope was dimmed when hatred soon reared its ugly head.

On the cold Denver night of February 5, 1970, eyewitnesses spotted three young white men scaling the fences at the school bus yard on the southern outskirts of the city. After entering the lot, the law-breakers placed a dozen dynamite bombs under the gas tanks of school vehicles and ignited the fuses. The series of explosions were heard a mile away. The firebombing totaled most of the vehicles marked for transporting Black students in the busing program. Still, one bus—number 13—survived. As luck would have it, I was among the few children given a seat on that bus.

I was seven years old and scheduled to start the first grade that fall. Every morning, I lined up with a small group of kids from my block on the side of the road, each of us carrying our schoolbooks and lunch boxes to wait for that lone bus, number 13. When I was transported to my new school, Carson Elementary, I entered a well-resourced school with excellent teachers.

I'll never forget the days I spent there. The educators at Carson welcomed me with open arms, challenging me to think critically and eliciting my full potential. At Carson, my experiences in a majority-white classroom taught me I can compete with anyone regardless of skin color. I was even named the "Outstanding Boy" for my grade, a source of immense pride as a young kid.

While everything seemed to progress positively at my new school, a tragedy befell our community on the other side of the district. Our family had a friend named Roosevelt. Personable and hardworking, Roosevelt had just finished his master's degree at Colorado State University and secured a prominent state job, a big deal back then for a Black person. My parents hadn't gotten their doctorates yet, and Roosevelt inspired them to do so.

One day, Roosevelt used his state credit card at a gas station. The attendant was so shocked that a Black man could possess a government charge card that he assumed Roosevelt had stolen it and shot and killed him. In our community, Roosevelt had been a symbol of success, an embodiment of what one could aspire to become. He had done everything right—gotten an education, built a distinguished career, and was a well-liked and upstanding citizen. Nonetheless, Roosevelt's life was taken by racism, echoing the violence in Tulsa that my ancestors had fled. Roosevelt's death devastated my family and our community.

At my school on the other side of the district, however, nobody seemed to know or care about his death. I was struck that while my new school recognized me as an Outstanding Boy, they seemed oblivious to the murder of an exceptional Black man.

Later on, I visited the house of a white schoolmate. It was one of my first times inside a white person's home. It really opened my eyes. His house was four times the size of ours. I couldn't comprehend it. His father worked as a contractor, and his mother was a homemaker. My dad had just earned his doctorate, but my schoolmate's father had only completed high school. My family, with two working parents, was significantly outearned by a less-educated white family with one income. Unfortunately, this hasn't changed much over the years: African American college graduates today have lower average net worth than white high school graduates.

As time passed, I experienced more of these contrasts, watching my white friends take ski trips to Aspen and vacations to Disneyland that my parents couldn't afford. Mom and Dad taught me to work hard and do well at school as a kid. But I started to see that, while those values were crucial, things weren't that simple.

Roosevelt's tragic death and my eye-opening visit to my white friend's home awakened me to the fact that there are often two economies, two justice systems, two sets of rules, two career tracks, and two standards of living. One for white Americans. The other for Black Americans. One group surfs the rising tide of privilege; the other swims against the riptide of racism. Dr. King spoke of these two realities in terms of both civil rights and economic opportunities. He described one America overflowing with "milk and honey" and another America where Black people live in dilapidated housing, send their children to substandard schools, and remain trapped in a cycle of poverty and unemployment.

These two Americas endure. Black Americans have been systematically denied participation in America's most significant economic opportunities. Land booms, the cotton boom, and the oil boom in America all excluded Black people. Due to the cancellation of land grant programs during and after Reconstruction, redlining, and racism in the housing market, the majority of Black people haven't owned a home since Emancipation. Rampant racist policies and practices in employment and education have yielded widespread racial disparities. These disparities reveal one America of promise and another where opportunities are few, hard-fought, and fleeting.

When we examine the research on our nation's few attempts to reduce or eliminate racial disparities—like Reconstruction, the short-lived busing era, affirmative action, and the push for more diversity in corporate America—we find that the benefits to African Americans were significant before the initiatives were halted. Regarding bused children, the institutions they attended were often generally better resourced, including better-stocked libraries, smaller class sizes, and more extracurricular activities.

Benefitting from such amenities, many bused students pursued higher-paying careers in business and the public sector with increased skill and confidence as adults and less aversion to environments where they were underrepresented. The kids in my community who weren't bused and went to lower-resourced schools had vastly different outcomes than those of us who were.

Decades later, disparities in education are still leaving too many kids without the opportunity to meet their educational needs. School districts serving predominantly Black communities spend $773 less per student yearly. After high school, African American kids are less likely to matriculate to college. Only 27 percent of Black Americans hold college degrees, compared to 41 percent of their white counterparts.

Following the termination of affirmative action in college admission by the Supreme Court in 2023, Black high school seniors now face a steeper challenge to be admitted into our country's best universities.

Unfortunately, while Black Americans are more likely to attend under-resourced schools and less likely to graduate from college, assaults on equality in education continue. In June 2023, the United States Supreme Court struck down affirmative action for college admissions, leading to a reported decline in African American enrollment at Ivy League schools and other elite colleges. For instance, the University of Amherst and MIT saw their enrollments of Black, Latino and Latina, and Indigenous students drop from 24 percent to 11 percent and 31 percent to 17 percent, respectively, while Tufts, Yale, and Princeton reported smaller but significant declines, according to admissions data from the colleges. In 2024, Harvard Law School admitted just nineteen Black first-year students, making up a mere 3.4 percent of the incoming class. This was a sharp decline from the previous year, when forty-three Black students were admitted. Some schools are experimenting with measures like free tuition or admission priority for low-income students in an effort to boost diversity, but the early numbers after the end of affirmative action are cause for concern.

Looking beyond admissions, the burden of financing higher education is often insurmountable. African American college students borrow nearly double the amount in student loans that their white peers borrow, and Black borrowers are five times likelier to default. These higher debt loads, in combination with lower homeownership rates, translate to Black Americans having more liabilities and fewer assets (on average), which together result in African Americans having a net worth ten times less than whites (on average).

Like the kids in my neighborhood who weren't bused to a better-resourced school, people of color, especially African Americans, still face underrepresentation in prestigious white-collar fields like finance, technology, and the sciences. We can address this by better funding and supporting our education system to make every American school a well-resourced school. We need teachers, parents, coaches, mentors, and community members to foster self-esteem and confidence in all children and explicitly tell them *they are enough*: They can pursue any career they want when they grow up if they work hard, no matter where they come from or what they look like. We must also expose kids to different vocations, especially in STEM, through career days, extracurricular activities, and internships. Doing so will encourage more young people from diverse backgrounds to pursue promising careers, slowly carrying us all to a more equitable and brighter future.

When I reached the fifth grade in 1975, the Denver busing program ended. Busing programs had faced significant pushback from white communities, leading to "white flight" and the politicization of the school zoning process. In 1974, a year before I left Carson, the Supreme Court limited the scope of school busing programs in the case of *Milliken v. Bradley*, which outlawed busing students across district lines. However, those five years of attending a better-resourced school profoundly impacted my life.

I still maintain contact with many students who were with me on bus 13. Remarkably, almost all of us became professionals, including elected officials, doctors, lawyers, engineers, teachers, community organizers, and business leaders. Our peers who were limited to lesser-resourced schools did not fare as well. We grew up together but lived in different worlds. My realization of the disparities between the two Americas, deepened by King's teachings, taught me the importance of discerning opportunities within a system while recognizing its shortcomings. While education was valued in my community and provided pathways to success for some, it wasn't equally accessible to all. This awareness drives me to seize opportunities while advocating for broader access and inclusivity—to lift as I climb.

Dr. King reminds us of our power to make a difference in the communities we care about. How will you embrace that power to create lasting change?

Dr. King at the end of the Montgomery Bus Boycott, Montgomery, Alabama, December 26, 1956.

Don Cravens / Getty Images

CHAPTER

4

Economic Justice

"The Three Evils of Society"

r. Chairman, friends, and brothers in this first gathering of the National Conference on New Politics. Ladies and gentlemen . . . can you hear me in the back? (No)

I don't know if the Klan is in here tonight or not with all the troubles we're having with these microphones. Seldom if ever . . . has. . . . we're still working with it.

As I was about to say, seldom if ever has such a diverse and truly ecumenical gathering convened under the egis of politics in our nation, and I want to commend the leadership of the National Conference on New Politics for all of the great work that they have done in making this significant convention possible. Indeed by our very nature we affirm that something new is taking place on the American political horizon.

We have come here from the dusty plantations of the Deep South and the depressing ghettos of the North. We have come from the great universities and the flourishing suburbs. We have come from Appalachian poverty and from conscience-stricken wealth. But we have come. And we have come here because we share a common concern for the moral health of our nation. We have come because our eyes have seen through the superficial glory and glitter of our society and observed the coming of judgment. Like the prophet of old, we have read the handwriting on the wall. We have seen our nation weighed in the balance of history and found wanting. We have come because we see this as a dark hour in the affairs of men. For most of us this is a new mood. We are traditionally the idealists. We are the marchers from Mississippi and Selma and Washington, who staked our lives on the American dream during the first half of this decade. Many assembled here campaigned lasciviously for Lyndon Johnson in 1964 because we could not stand idly by and watch our nation contaminated by the eighteenth-century policies of Goldwaterism. We were the hardcore activists who were willing to believe that Southerners could be reconstructed in the constitutional image. We were the dreamers of a dream that dark yesterdays of man's inhumanity to man would soon be transformed into bright tomorrows of justice. Now it is hard to escape the disillusionment and betrayal. Our hopes have been blasted and our dreams have been shattered.

The promise of a Great Society was shipwrecked off the coast of Asia, on the dreadful peninsula of Vietnam. The poor, Black and white, are still perishing on a lonely island of poverty in the midst of a vast ocean of material prosperity. What happens to a dream deferred? It leads to bewildering frustration and corroding bitterness. I came to see this in a personal experience here in Chicago last summer. In all the speaking I have done in the United States before varied audiences, including some hostile whites, the only time I have ever been booed was one night in our regular weekly mass meetings by some angry young men of our movement.

Now I went home that night with an ugly feeling. Selfishly I thought of my suffering and sacrifices over the last twelve years. Why would they boo one so close to them? But as I lay awake thinking, I finally came to myself. And I could not for the life of me have less impatience and understanding for those young men. For twelve years, I and others like me have held out radiant promises of progress. I had preached to them about my dream. I had lectured to them about the not-too-distant day when they would have freedom, all here, now. I had urged them to have faith in America and in white society. Their hopes had soared. They were now booing me because they felt that we were unable to deliver on our promises. They were booing because we had urged them to have faith in people who had too often proved to be unfaithful. They were now hostile because they were watching the dream that they had so readily accepted turn into a frustrating nightmare. This situation is all the more ominous in view of the rising expectations of men the world over. The deep rumbling that we hear today, the rumblings of discontent, is the thunder of disinherited masses rising from dungeons of oppression to the bright hills of freedom. All over the world like a fever, freedom is spreading in the widest liberation movement in history. The great masses of people are determined to end the exploitation of their races and lands. And in one majestic chorus they are singing in the words of our freedom song, "Ain't gonna let nobody turn us around."

And so the collision course is set. The people cry for freedom and the congress attempts to legislate repression. Millions, yes billions, are appropriated for mass murder; but the most meager pittance for foreign aid for international development is crushed in the surge of reaction. Unemployment rages at a major depression level in the Black ghettos, but the bipartisan response is an anti-riot bill rather than a serious poverty program. The modest proposals for model cities, rent supplement, and rat control, pitiful as they were to begin with, get caught in the maze of congressional inaction. And I submit to you tonight, that a congress that proves to be more anti-Negro than anti-rat needs to be dismissed.

It seems that our legislative assemblies have adopted Nero as their patron saint and are bent on fiddling while our cities burn. Even when the people persist and in the face of great obstacles develop indigenous leadership and self-help approaches to their problems and finally tread the forest of bureaucracy to obtain existing government funds, the corrupt political order seeks to crush even this beginning of hope. The case of CDGM in Mississippi is the most publicized example but it is a story repeated many times across our nation. Our own experience here in Chicago is especially painfully present. After an enthusiastic approval by HEW's Department of Adult Education, SCLC began an adult literacy project to aid one thousand young men and women who have been pushed out of overcrowded ghetto schools, in obtaining basic [literacy] skills prerequisite to receiving jobs.

We had an agreement with A&P stores for 750 jobs through SCLC's job program, Operation Breadbasket, and had recruited over five hundred pupils the first week. At that point Congressman Paccinski and the Daley machine intervened and demanded that Washington cut off our funds or channel them through the machine-controlled poverty program in Chicago. Now we have no problem with administrative supervision, but we do have a desire to be independent of machine control and the Democratic Party patronage network. For this desire for a politically independent approach to the needs of our brothers, our funds are being stopped as of September 15 and a very meaningful program discontinued.

Yes the hour is dark; evil comes forth in the guise of good. It is a time of double talk when men in high places have a high blood pressure of deceptive rhetoric and an anemia of concrete performance. We cry out against welfare handouts to the poor but generously approve an oil depletion allowance to make the rich richer. Six Mississippi plantations receive more than a million dollars a year not to plant cotton, but no provision is made to feed the tenant farmer who is put out of work by the government subsidy.

The crowning achievement in hypocrisy must go to those staunch Republicans and Democrats of the Midwest and West, who were given land by our government when they came here as immigrants from Europe. They were given education through the land grant colleges. They were provided with agricultural agents to keep them abreast of forming trends, they were granted low-interest loans to aid in the mechanization of their farms, and now that they have succeeded in becoming successful, they are paid not to farm, and these are the same people that now say to Black people, whose ancestors were brought to this country in chains and who were emancipated in 1863 without being given land to cultivate or bread to eat, that they must pull themselves up by their own bootstraps. What they truly advocate is socialism for the rich and capitalism for the poor.

I wish that I could say that this is just a passing phase in the cycles of our nation's life; certainly times of war, times of reaction throughout the society, but I suspect that we are now experiencing the coming to the surface of a triple-pronged sickness that has been lurking within our body politic from its very beginning. That is the sickness of racism, excessive materialism, and militarism. Not only is this our nation's dilemma; it is the plague of Western civilization. As early as 1906 W. E. B. Dubois prophesied that the problem of the twentieth century would be the problem of the color line; now as we stand two-thirds into this crucial period of history we know full well that racism is still that hound of hell which dogs the tracks of our civilization.

Ever since the birth of our nation, white America has had a schizophrenic personality on the question of race. She has been torn between selves. A self in which she proudly professes the great principle of democracy and a self in which she madly practices the antithesis of democracy. This tragic duality has produced a strange indecisiveness and ambivalence toward the Negro, causing America to take a step backwards simultaneously with every step forward on the question of racial justice; to be at once attracted to the Negro and repelled by him, to love and to hate him. There has never been a solid, unified, and determined thrust to make justice a reality for Afro-Americans.

The step backwards has a new name today. It is called the white backlash, but the white backlash is nothing new. It is the surfacing of old prejudices, hostilities, and ambivalences that have always been there. It was caused neither by the cry of "Black power" nor by the unfortunate recent wave of riots in our cities. The white backlash of today is rooted in the same problem that has characterized America ever since the Black man landed in chains on the shores of this nation.

This does not imply that all white Americans are racist, far from it. Many white people have, through a deep moral compulsion, fought long and hard for racial justice. Nor does it mean that America has made no progress in her attempt to cure the body politic of the disease of racism or that the dogma of racism has not been considerably modified in recent years. However, for the good of America, it is necessary to refute the idea that the dominant ideology in our country, even today, is freedom and equality while racism is just an occasional departure from the norm on the part of a few bigoted extremists.

Racism can well be that corrosive evil that will bring down the curtain on Western civilization. Arnold Toynbee has said that some twenty-six civilizations have risen upon the face of the earth, and almost all of them have descended into the junk heap of destruction. The decline and fall of these civilizations, according to Toynbee, was not caused by external invasion but by internal decay. They failed to respond creatively to the challenges impingent upon them.

If America does not respond creatively to the challenge to banish racism, some future historian will have to say that a great civilization died because it lacked the soul and commitment to make justice a reality for all men.

The second aspect of our afflicted society is extreme materialism. An Asian writer has portrayed our dilemma in candid terms. He says, "You call your thousand material devices labor saving machinery, yet you are forever busy. With the multiplying of your machinery, you grow increasingly fatigued, anxious, nervous, dissatisfied. Whatever you have you want more and wherever you are you want to go somewhere else. Your devices are neither time saving nor soul saving machinery. They are so many sharp spurs which urge you on to invent more machinery and to do more business."

This tells us something about our civilization that cannot be cast aside as a prejudiced charge by an Eastern thinker who is jealous of Western prosperity. We cannot escape the indictment. This does not mean that we must turn back the clock of scientific progress. No one can overlook the wonders that science has wrought for our lives. The automobile will not abdicate in favor of the horse and buggy or the train in favor of the stagecoach or the tractor in favor of the hand plow or the scientific method in favor of ignorance and superstition.

But our moral lag must be redeemed; when scientific power outruns moral power, we end up with guided missiles and misguided men. When we foolishly maximize the minimum and minimize the maximum we sign the warrant for our own day of doom. It is this moral lag in our thing-oriented society that blinds us to the human reality around us and encourages us in the greed and exploitation which creates the sector of poverty in the midst of wealth.

Again we have deluded ourselves into believing the myth that capitalism grew and prospered out of the protestant ethic of hard work and sacrifice. The fact is that capitalism was built on the exploitation and suffering of Black slaves and continues to thrive on the exploitation of the poor—both Black and white, both here and abroad. If Negroes and poor whites do not participate in the free flow of wealth within our economy, they will forever be poor, giving their energies, their talents, and their limited funds to the consumer market but reaping few benefits and services in return.

The way to end poverty is to end the exploitation of the poor; ensure them a fair share of the government services and the nation's resources. I proposed recently that a national agency be established to provide employment for everyone needing it. Nothing is more socially inexcusable than unemployment in this age. In the thirties, when the nation was bankrupt it instituted such an agency, the WPA. In the present conditions of a nation glutted with resources, it is barbarous to condemn people desiring work to soul-sapping inactivity and poverty. I am convinced that even this one massive act of concern will do more than all the state police and armies of the nation to quell riots and still hatreds.

The tragedy is our materialistic culture does not possess the statesmanship necessary to do it. Victor Hugo could have been thinking of twentieth-century America when he wrote, "there's always more misery among the lower classes than there is humanity in the higher classes."

The time has come for America to face the inevitable choice between materialism and humanism. We must devote at least as much to our children's education and the health of the poor as we do to the care of our automobiles and the building of beautiful, impressive hotels. We must also realize that the problems of racial injustice and economic injustice cannot be solved without a radical redistribution of political and economic power.

We must further recognize that the ghetto is a domestic colony. Black people must develop programs that will aid in the transfer of power and wealth into the hands of residents of the ghetto so that they may in reality control their own destinies. This is the meaning of New Politics. People of will in the larger community must support the Black man in this effort.

The final phase of our national sickness is the disease of militarism. Nothing more clearly demonstrates our nation's abuse of military power than our tragic adventure in Vietnam. This war has played havoc with the destiny of the entire world. It has torn up the Geneva Agreement, it has seriously impaired the United Nations, it has exacerbated the hatred between continents and worse still between races. It has frustrated our development at home, telling our own underprivileged citizens that we place insatiable military demands above their critical needs. It has greatly contributed to the forces of reaction in America and strengthened the military-industrial complex. And it has practically destroyed Vietnam and left thousands of American and Vietnamese youth maimed and mutilated and exposed the whole world to the risk of nuclear warfare. Above all, the war in Vietnam has revealed what Senator Fulbright calls "our nation's arrogance of power."

We are arrogant in professing to be concerned about the freedom of foreign nations while not setting our own house in order. Many of our senators and congressmen vote joyously to appropriate billions of dollars for the war in Vietnam, and many of these same senators and congressmen vote loudly against a fair housing bill to make it possible for a Negro veteran of Vietnam to purchase a decent home. We arm Negro soldiers to kill on foreign battlefields but offer little protection for their relatives from beatings and killings in our own South. We are willing to make a Negro 100 percent of a citizen in warfare but reduce him to 50 percent of a citizen on American soil.

No war in our nation's history has ever been so violative of our conscience, our national interest, and so destructive of our moral standing before the world. No enemy has ever been able to cause such damage to us as we inflict upon ourselves.

The inexorable decay of our urban centers has flared into terrifying domestic conflict as the pursuit of foreign war absorbs our wealth and energy. Squalor and poverty scar our cities as our military might destroy cities in a far-off land to support oligarchy, to intervene in domestic conflict. The president who cherishes consensus for peace has intensified the war in answer to a cry to stop the war. It has brought tauntingly to one minute's flying time from China to a moment before the midnight of world conflagration. We are offered a tax for war instead of a plan for peace. Men of reason should no longer debate the merits of war or means of financing war. They should end the war and restore sanity and humanity to American policy. And if the will of the people continues to be unheeded, all men of goodwill must create a situation in which the 1967–68 elections are made a referendum on the war. The American people must have an opportunity to vote into oblivion those who cannot detach themselves from militarism, and those that lead us.

So we are here because we believe, we hope, we pray that something new might emerge in the political life of this nation which will produce a new man, new structures and institutions, and a new life for mankind. I am convinced that this new life will not emerge until our nation undergoes a radical revolution of values. When machines and computers, profit motives and property rights, are considered more important than people, the giant triplets of racism, economic exploitation, and militarism are incapable of being conquered. A civilization can flounder as readily in the face of moral bankruptcy as it can through financial bankruptcy.

A true revolution of values will soon cause us to question the fairness and justice of many of our past and present policies. We are called to play the Good Samaritan on life's roadside, but that will only be an initial act. One day the whole Jericho Road must be transformed so that men and women will not be beaten and robbed as they make their journey through life. True compassion is more than flinging a coin to a beggar; it understands that an edifice which produces beggars needs restructuring.

A true revolution of values will soon look uneasily on the glaring contrast of poverty and wealth. With righteous indignation it will look at thousands of working people displaced from their jobs, with reduced incomes as a result of automation while the profits of the employers remain intact, and say, "This is not just."

It will look across the ocean and see individual capitalists of the West investing huge sums of money in Asia and Africa, only to take the profits out with no concern for the social betterment of the countries, and say, "This is not just."

It will look at our alliance with the landed gentry of Latin America and say, "This is not just."

A true revolution of values will lay hands on the world order and say of war, "This way of settling differences is not just."

This business of burning human being with napalm, of filling our nation's home with orphans and widows, of injecting poisonous drugs of hate into the veins of peoples normally humane, of sending men home from dark and bloodied battlefields physically handicapped and psychologically deranged cannot be reconciled with wisdom, justice, and love.

A nation that continues year after year to spend more money on military defense than on programs of social uplift is approaching spiritual death.

So what we must all see is that these are revolutionary times. All over the globe, men are revolting against old systems of exploitation, and out of the wombs of a frail world, new systems of justice and equality are being born. The shirtless and barefoot of the earth are rising up as never before. The people who sat in darkness have seen a great light. We in the West must support these revolutions. It is a sad fact that because of comfort, complacency, a morbid fear of communism, and our proneness to adjust to injustice, the Western nations that initiated so much of the revolutionary spirit of the modern world have now become the arch anti-revolutionaries.

This has driven many to feel that only Marxism has the revolutionary spirit. In a sense, communism is a judgment of our failure to make democracy real and to follow through on the revolutions that we initiated. Our only hope today lies in our ability to recapture the revolutionary spirit and go out into a sometimes hostile world, declaring eternal opposition to poverty, racism, and militarism. With this powerful commitment, we shall boldly challenge the status quo and unjust mores and thereby speed the day when every valley shall be exalted and every mountain and hill shall be made low and the crooked places shall be made straight and the rough places plain.

May I say in conclusion that there is a need now, more than ever before, for men and women in our nation to be creatively maladjusted. Mr. Davis said and I say to you that I choose to be among the maladjusted. As my good friend Bill Coffin said, there are those who have criticized me and many of you for taking a stand against the war in Vietnam and for seeking to say to the nation that the issues of civil rights cannot be separated from the issues of peace.

I want to say to you tonight that I intend to keep these issues mixed because they are mixed. Somewhere we must see that justice is indivisible, injustice anywhere is a threat to justice everywhere, and I have fought too long and too hard against segregated public accommodations to end up at this point in my life segregating my moral concerns.

So let us stand in this convention knowing that on some positions, cowardice asks the question, Is it safe? Expediency asks the question, Is it politic? Vanity asks the question, Is it popular? But conscience asks the question, Is it right? And on some positions, it is necessary for the moral individual to take a stand that is neither safe, nor politic, nor popular. But he must do it because it is right. And we say to our nation tonight, we say to our government, we even say to our FBI, "We will not be harassed, we will not make a butchery of our conscience, we will not be intimidated, and we will be heard."

—Dr. Martin Luther King Jr.

August 31, 1967, the National Conference on New Politics, Chicago, Illinois

In "The Three Evils of Society," Dr. King highlighted how three factors—racism, poverty, and militarism—fuel racial inequality. Racist ideas drive hiring discrimination and limit access to education and capital, perpetuating the racial wealth gap. As Dr. King said, "We are called to play the Good Samaritan . . . but . . . one day the whole Jericho Road must be transformed." To build a just society, we must transform these systems by creating equitable access to education, entrepreneurship, and wealth generation.

Months after the inaugural celebration of Martin Luther King Jr. Day as a national holiday in 1986, I graduated from Cornell University with a degree in chemical engineering. After leaving campus, I worked at an industrial complex on a flat stretch of land in Upstate New York, about a mile from the Niagara River. As a first-year engineer, I spent long hours toiling in a windowless office inside a production facility. I wasn't there long before I noticed I was only one of four Black employees at the worksite, and the other three were shift workers. They were all men who toiled in a sweltering area of the plant, handling and pouring high-temperature molten compounds that are now known to cause bladder, kidney, and liver cancer. It was hazardous and strenuous manual labor. One day there was an accident where the scorching slurry was spilled, burning three-quarters of the skin off one of the brothers' backs. That grisly incident stayed with me.

Later, I was installing a system at a pulp mill in Pine Bluff, Arkansas, where there were only about half a dozen African Americans out of more than three hundred workers. These Black workers were assigned to two areas with the highest concentration of dangerous gasses being released. Throughout my engineering career, it became part of a pattern that would play out at seemingly every place I went: Black employees were underrepresented in the head count, and those who got hired often seemed to be placed in the most dangerous roles. It was painful to witness. I had hoped things had improved since I was a child, when I overheard my parents and friends complain about having lower pay and less opportunity than their white counterparts.

However, what I witnessed as a young engineer in industrial settings confirmed that we hadn't yet reached racial economic justice. In addition to higher levels of occupational injuries and fatalities, African American workers still have, on average, lower wages and higher unemployment than white workers. Smaller paychecks result in lower living standards, including worse health outcomes; less money to spend on education; and lower savings, investments, and business formation rates. These factors all compound with historical inequities to create a racial wealth gap as wide as the river canyons in Colorado, where I grew up.

Economic disparities are often passed down from parent to child, beginning in the early years of a child's life and following them through adulthood. A critical factor in economic outcomes is where people grow up. African American children are less likely to reside in family-owned homes and less likely to live in educational districts with well-resourced schools. Today, 45 percent of Black families own a home versus 73 percent of whites, partly due to a lack of affordable housing and a long history of racist lending policies. If Black families own their properties, they often have lower values due to the legacy of redlining and the current racist practices in appraisals. I think about the well-maintained homes my peers and I lived in growing up and how they appraised at maybe half what similar homes in white areas of Denver did.

The housing boom of the past century has been the greatest wealth-creating phenomenon in American history. As in the previous booms, African Americans were not fully included. It's important to remember that in the cotton boom of the nineteenth century, Black people were exploited as enslaved labor while plantation owners became millionaires. So did oil drillers and speculators during the American Gusher Age at the turn of the twentieth century, which often banned Black people from energy jobs. Black people have had lower land ownership rates since the land grant programs established during Reconstruction were rescinded. Unfortunately, the lack of equal access to participate in America's real estate booms persists today.

The current affordable housing crisis is hitting Black areas particularly hard, resulting in lower homeownership rates, a declining standard of living, and a high rent burden rate among minorities. Lower homeownership rates mean there's little family wealth to invest in education, start-ups, or businesses. As a result of a lack of participation in previous booms, African Americans can't roll accumulated resources into the next opportunity. For example, instead of being able to tap home equity accumulated during the twentieth-century property boom to pay for their children's educations—degrees that will be needed to participate in the tech boom—many Black families are forced to use student loans to pay for education. Today, student loan payments consume 10 percent more of Black borrowers' wealth-building capital than they do for whites, perpetuating a cycle of lower household wealth for African Americans.

When minorities enter the workforce after being raised in households with lower family wealth, struggling to access a suitable education, and often having crushing student loan debt, they usually face employment racism, adding insult to injury. In studies, résumés with "Black-sounding" names, for example, are less likely to result in an invitation for interviews. There is often a hesitancy to hire qualified

Black job applicants, resulting in an underrepresentation of Black people in white-collar professions, even when accounting for differences in educational attainment. Like the Black men I worked with in various factories when I was an engineer, blue-collar job seekers often have to take dangerous or dead-end roles. Given all these headwinds, it's unsurprising that the Black unemployment rate is nearly double that of whites. The Black-white wage gap has grown since the 1970s. Currently, white workers earn almost 25 percent more than Black workers.

In response to employment, wage suppression, and poor working conditions, Black Americans who migrated to industrial centers as part of the Great Migration turned to organized labor in the 1940s and 1950s. Union participation has been a point of pride for African Americans ever since. One of the civil rights movement's co-architects, A. Philip Randolph, cut his teeth in the labor movement as head of the Pullman Porters Union and later the American Federation of Labor and Congress of Industrial Organizations (AFL-CIO). And, memorably, Dr. King's last speech was to striking janitors in 1968.

Despite the importance of Black organized labor, Black fund managers rarely oversee the pension funds of workers, a stark contrast given that Black Americans are more likely to be union members than any other racial group. Only around 2 percent of fund managers are Black, while African Americans are roughly 11 percent of pension holders. This underrepresentation has far-reaching consequences, as some investments harm marginalized communities and contribute to gentrification and displacement.

Business ownership is another arena marked by under-representation. The entrepreneurial spirit within African American communities has deep historical roots, dating back to freedmen during the antebellum era who often operated as self-employed cooks, caterers, or barbers. The spirit of entrepreneurship, do-for-self, and hustling persists today, so why isn't it translating into business formation? Chiefly because there is a pressing need for greater access to capital.

Communities of color are more likely to be underbanked, hindering folks' ability to establish relationships with lending institutions. When Black Americans apply for loans to start or expand their businesses, they face lower approval rates and higher average interest rates.

Despite the entrepreneurial zeal that permeates Black culture, the quest for equitable access to capital remains a formidable uphill battle.

In recent years, Community Development Financial Institutions (CDFIs) have emerged as a potential solution for getting capital into underbanked communities like Black enclaves. Historically, the banking gap was filled by Black-owned banks. Still, these vital institutions have begun to disappear in recent decades. Between 1888 and 1934, there were 134 Black-owned banks. Today, regrettably, only 20 remain. As a result of disparities in branch bank options, more than one in four African Americans are underbanked. The lack of banks in our communities makes building wealth more difficult. It becomes a struggle to secure a mortgage or a business loan, resulting in borrowers facing higher loan denial rates and paying higher interest rates on loans, due in no small part to a lack of competition among lenders for their business.

CDFIs are specialized organizations that focus on bridging the capital-access gap for communities with low branch density. They provide vital financial services, including small business loans, mortgages, microloans, economic aid, and investments in community development projects. Recently, a legislative push has been made to increase federal funding for CDFIs. However, as we've seen repeatedly throughout history, the program's structure threatens to exclude many Black Americans.

The federal funds allocated to CDFIs have primarily gone to digitized ones, meaning they use industry-standard fintech software and offer online transactions and services. However, the CDFIs that work in majority-Black Southern communities like Memphis and Birmingham are digitized at a much lower rate. Therefore, the bulk of African American communities have not experienced the full impact of the increase in federal funding to CDFIs. I have been highlighting this issue to the public officials overseeing these programs while helping CDFIs in Black communities to digitize and acquire the latest software. Still, policy changes are needed to ensure African Americans are fully included.

When I think about this issue, I think about the lessons we should have learned from the inequitable structure of the New Deal programs and the GI Bill. The GI Bill funded programs for job training, education, home loans, and healthcare for veterans after World War II, but Black Americans were less likely than white Americans to be beneficiaries. The GI Bill's federally allocated funds were sent to the states to administer. In the South, many locales intentionally gave African Americans the short shrift. In some instances, Black veterans were denied the same educational and vocational training as white vets. Through redlining, many Black borrowers were denied loans for homes in preferred areas.

Today, the federal government has earmarked $42.25 billion in funding for Broadband Equity, Access, and Deployment (BEAD) Program to expand broadband access. However, like the GI Bill, the states have a say over how the broadband funds will be spent. Regrettably, many southern states—some of the same ones that cut Black veterans out of the GI programs—have not included African Americans in the process of developing the plans for broadband installation in their BEAD grant applications. I can't underscore how much access to general-purpose technologies like broadband and artificial intelligence will be pivotal in allowing Americans to participate in the coming technology boom in artificial intelligence, robotics, the Internet of Things, Web3, blockchain, 3D printing, genetic engineering, and quantum computing. These sectors will create millions of new jobs and business opportunities. However, with 40 percent of African Americans currently without access to adequate high-speed internet, Black Americans could be cut out of this fourth significant economic expansion in American history like they were with the first three. That's why when I saw this process unfolding and began compiling data about the needs of communities, particularly those around Historically Black Colleges and Universities (HBCUs), I ensured this was shared with the states in the hope that broadband development would occur equitably. I've also liaised with the federal government to underscore how important it is that this is not another GI Bill where everyone, besides African Americans, is included in receiving broadband grants.

Similarly, in 2021, the Department of Education proclaimed that institutions that still needed to meet specific cybersecurity benchmarks would lose their ability to receive Title IV funding, including the most common forms of financial aid such as Pell Grants and direct loans. This threatened to disproportionately disrupt higher learning for African Americans, as most HBCUs had no way to meet these requirements on time and found themselves on the brink of losing access to Title IV funding. Notably, around 80 percent of HBCU students depended on these federal student aid programs. I knew the consequences would be dire if these HBCUs lost access to most financial aid.

So, I took proactive measures through my nonprofit, the Student

Freedom Initiative. I orchestrated fundraising efforts and personally injected funds to swiftly bolster cybersecurity measures in these institutions, ensuring they met the requisite standards to safeguard their funding. We protected sixty-one HBCUs and preserved over $1.5 billion annually in Title IV funds that would have otherwise gone away from our HBCUs. These incidents reflect the fact that we have not fully learned from our country's history of excluding African Americans during economic expansions; the issues with BEAD and Title IV funding are reminders that African Americans will only be fully included in the tech boom if we push for it.

The next wave of general-purpose technologies is artificial intelligence. For the African American community to fully engage with the transformative impact of these tools, access is essential. But equally important is ensuring that these AI models are free from the biases that could disproportionately harm our community. One powerful way to guarantee equitable access is through initiatives like the AI coursework introduced at Morehouse and Spelman by Stats Perform, which became the most popular class last year. Additionally, it's critical that those developing these technologies provide access to resources and training throughout the build-out phase. The fight for equity in AI is not just about access—it's about ensuring that these systems are designed with our values in mind. This is a reminder of our collective power to make a real difference in the communities we care about. Embrace that power, and let it drive the change we wish to see.

I see economic justice as Martin Luther King Jr.'s unfulfilled legacy. In his last years before his life was cut short, he called attention to many of the issues I've discussed—the lack of adequate schools, higher unemployment, lack of proper housing, and poor access to healthcare—as part of his final initiative, the Poor People's Campaign. He memorably said that we need "a new kind of Selma or Birmingham to dramatize the economic plight of the Negro, and compel the government to act." It's a shame he was taken from us before he got to finish that work.

So where do we go from here, and where is Dr. King's proverbial mountaintop as we endeavor to ascend to economic justice? The good news is that this is an opportune time to address economic justice. We are at the precipice of another tremendous wealth-generating event: the rapidly growing tech sector. Imagine if African Americans are fully included in the technology boom. It would get us closer to the economic justice Dr. King envisioned.

I founded the Southern Communities Initiative (SCI) to put these solutions into action. The SCI is a collective of corporate and philanthropic partners committed to funding and implementing solutions to drive racial and economic equality in the six cities where more than half of all African Americans live: Atlanta, Birmingham, Charlotte, Houston, Memphis, and Greater New Orleans. We are dedicated to supporting projects that bring financial resources and training to enhance wealth formation, homeownership, small businesses, and careers in tech.

In the grander scheme, assisting African Americans in accessing the digital realm and equipping them with the skills and capital necessary to compete in the forthcoming technologically driven era doesn't provide an instant panacea for closing the racial wealth gap. However, it can be a significant stride toward a more equitable future, a chance far more promising than history has previously afforded us.

Dr. King's message of empathy and solidarity has pushed me to realize the importance of advocating for others and understanding the mechanisms in society that perpetuate economic injustice. I learned to observe, reflect, and be an ally, recognizing that progress requires active engagement and a commitment to challenging systemic inequalities.

As you identify gaps in access
to essential technologies, how
can you influence business
leaders and local politicians
to direct resources where they
are needed most? Dr. King
reminds us that we all have the
power to drive change. You'd
be surprised how responsive
stakeholders will be when you
reach out to draw attention
to these areas of need.

Dr. King with faith leaders Bishop James Shannon, Rabbi Abraham Joshua Heschel, and Rabbi Maurice Eisendrath at a protest at the Tomb of the Unknown Soldier in Arlington Cemetery, February 6, 1968.

CHAPTER

5

Allies

Address to the National Biennial Convention of the American Jewish Congress

It is a great pleasure to address an audience whose sympathy and understanding of a deep social problem of our age have boldly been expressed, and resolutely supported, by deeds and action. It is equally a pleasure to share the platform with Walter Reuther and Dr. Nahum Goldmann, who have both given wise and sincere leadership at home and abroad in the spirit of noble ideals implemented by dynamic and creative actions.

My people were brought to America in chains. Your people were driven here to escape the chains fashioned for them in Europe. Our unity is born of our common struggle for centuries, not only to rid ourselves of bondage, but to make oppression of any people by others an impossibility.

The story of freedom's struggle to emerge and root itself in our nation began not in one place, but in several. I would like to mention one of these early incidents quite familiar to you, but not known to many Americans.

In the first week of September 1654, twenty-three Jewish refugees from the Portuguese Inquisition arrived in New Amsterdam on board the sailing ship the *St. Charles*. This was the first ship of Jews to reach the New World as a community, though Jews were members of the crew of Christopher Columbus. Peter Stuyvesant, in a document which he described as "friendly," asked that these "hateful enemies and blasphemers" get out of the New World. The history of America might have been different had these twenty-three Jews retreated with a beaten spirit. Instead, they peacefully and in dignity asserted their moral and political right to remain to settle as equals and to contribute to the building of a new society. As the history of all ages teaches us, no autocrat can dismember or destroy an unfolding truth; and Peter Stuyvesant, with his powerful authority, was ultimately defeated by these twenty-three determined Jews, who remained and became a responsible part of New Amsterdam. The governor of Arkansas in this day faced nine Negro school children with the same bigotry and distrust as the hate-filled Peter Stuyvesant. They, too, will resist and win against all odds and thereby enlarge the democratic vistas of our nation in the same glowing traditions as the Jews of the *St. Charles*. Thus three hundred years apart, two struggles for democracy were waged as America still strives to "proclaim liberty throughout the world."

One of history's most despicable tyrants, Adolf Hitler, sought to redefine morality as a good exclusively for the Aryan race. He bathed mankind in oceans of blood, murdering millions of Jews, old and young, and even the unborn. Negroes saw that such hideous racism, though not immediately applied to them, must sooner or later encompass them, and willingly they supported the struggle to achieve his defeat.

There are Hitlers loose in America today, both in high and low places. As the tensions and bewilderment of economic problems become more severe, history's scapegoats, the Jews, will be joined by new scapegoats, the Negroes. The Hitlers will seek to divert people's minds and turn their frustrations and anger to the helpless, to the outnumbered. Then whether the Negro and Jew shall live in peace will depend upon how firmly they resist, how effectively they reach the minds of the decent Americans to halt this deadly diversion.

Every Negro leader is keenly aware, from direct and personal experience, that the segregationists make no fine distinctions between the Negro and the Jew. The irrational hatred motivating his actions is as readily turned against Catholic, Jew, Quaker, liberal, and one-worlder as it is against the Negro. Some have jeered at Jews with Negroes; some have bombed the homes and churches of Negroes; and in recent acts of inhuman barbarity, some have bombed your synagogues—indeed, right here in Florida. Have the Nazis murdered Catholic Poles and Jews, Protestant Norwegians and Jews? The races of America fly blindly at both of us, caring not at all which of us falls. Their aim is to maintain through cruel segregation groups whose uses as scapegoats can facilitate their political and social rule over all people. Our common fight is against these deadly enemies of democracy, and our glory is that we are chosen to prove that courage is a characteristic of oppressed people, however cynically and brutally they are denied full equality and freedom.

I do not believe the American people, including the decent-minded people of the South really want two social classes in a grotesque democracy. They have been misled, their fears aroused, and their negative attitudes encouraged. But, as we together move forward in nonviolent pursuit of reasonable goals, the realization that injustice is being done must reveal itself.

Standing here in a Southern city before an audience of Southerners,

Northerners, Westerners, Christians, and Jews, I say, as I have said to hundreds of thousands of Negroes, that if the Southern white were freed of artificially contrived restraints, his instinctive will to fairness would bring him to oppose the racists. The forces of evil are a minority in this nation.

We, the Negroes, need some simple things in order to realize the huge potential. We need equal education, which the Supreme Court declared can only be realized if it is unsegregated. We need representative government so that the laws we legislate and obey are our own. We need economic opportunities so that we can bring up our families in security, encouraging our children to higher levels of education with the assurance that it can be available. The wealthiest nation on earth can certainly afford this. The nation whose founders believed in democracy and equality can afford to give these without violating its principles or corrupting its culture. But these things are deliberately and forcibly withheld. Like the twenty-three Jews on the *St. Charles*, Negroes do not propose to re-embark and sail away because a few misguided bigots order us to do so. We say, as they did, that the vast majority of people are truly ready to open the doors of opportunity and will do so if permitted to express their will.

With this confidence, we are peacefully but insistently organizing ourselves to vote, to educate our children side by side with white children, and to seek fair employment practices. These are described by some as extremists' demands. They are distorted as concealing a real purpose—to intermarry, to establish Black supremacy, to introduce lawlessness. But all people of goodwill realize that these things are not our program. If employment, the franchise, education, and brotherhood are extremists' demands, then the Old and the New Testaments are wildly extremist documents. If these are extremist demands, then democracy, itself, is extremist and the world needs to reverse its course and move backwards to the age of monarchs and tyranny. A job, to vote, and education, a socially and friendly and relaxed community are not a wild dream of centuries in the future. Indeed, if our technologically brilliant age cannot provide these things, it stands on the brink of disaster, for they are the bare minimum of existence in an advancing world. What a bit of irony it is that we have in the past decade created machines that think and with them people who fear to think.

Specifically to you I ask that you give an example to liberals by speaking out boldly. Today we are finding, too often, a quasi liberalism which is committed to the principle of looking sympathetically at all sides. It is a liberalism so objectively analytical that it fails to become subjectively committed. It is a liberalism which has developed a high blood pressure of words and an anemia of deeds. You can, with your community organization experience, assist in the development of platforms from which white moderates, liberals, and others may speak and act toward effective ends. Let us both realize that history has thrust upon us an indescribably important destiny—to complete a process of democratization which our nation has developed too slowly, but which is our most powerful weapon for world respect and emulation.

The shape of the world today does not permit us the luxury of an anemic democracy. Consider the monumental impact of this truth. The so-called backward nation of India, the jungle-fringed islands of Indonesia, in Burma and in nations of Africa, there is a freer franchise than in the Southland of the United States. In Mississippi, a Negro college professor is turned away from the polls and a minister is shot and killed for attempting to vote, but in India, an illiterate, penniless peasant is provided with a special ballot so his vote may fairly be recorded. The contrast in this practice of democracy may escape many Americans. It does not escape Indians. This may explain why our dazzling wealth and profuse rhetoric of democratic principles leave them unimpressed.

The new South which is emerging is not something that will come into being devoid of human effort. Human progress is neither automatic nor inevitable. Even a superficial look at history reveals that no level of human progress goes in on the wheels of inevitability. Rather, it seems clear that every step towards the goals of justice and freedom requires sacrifice, suffering, and struggle. Social progress is never attained by passive waiting. It comes only through the tireless efforts and passionate concern of dedicated individuals. Without this persistent work, time itself becomes an ally of the insurgent and primitive forces of irrational emotionalism and social stagnation. So we are challenged to work indefatigably for the full realization of the dream of brotherhood and integration. This is no time for apathy nor complacency. This is a time for vigorous and positive action.

America, the first nation to electrify the world with a new concept of man's capability of self-rule without monarchs or regents, must fulfill the promises of its constitution and Declaration of Independence. Failing this, no power of nuclear weapons or limitless wealth can prevent the steady erosion and diminishing of its grandeur in a century of climactic changes.

—Dr. Martin Luther King Jr.

May 14, 1958, Address to the American Jewish Congress, Miami, Florida

Dr. King's 1958 speech to the American Jewish Congress was a call to action—inviting the Jewish community into the struggle for civil rights. Throughout his life Dr. King used coalition-building to unite African Americans, Jewish Americans, Catholics, Lantinx, and even Indian Gandhian activists to fight for civil rights. His example shows us how calling allies into the fight is pivotal in the march forward for justice.

Some time ago, I obtained an original program from 1963 from the March on Washington that I attended as an infant with my mother. It's a prized possession of mine. The white paper of the leaflet has faded to a yellow hue, but its black typeface is still crisp. The header reads in bold, "THE MARCH ON WASHINGTON FOR JOBS AND FREEDOM." The mantra "We Shall Overcome" is emblazoned at the bottom margin. The speakers are listed in the document's body. When I hold the aged leaflet in my hands and examine it, my eye takes in the names of African American luminaries who spoke that day: John Lewis, Joseph Abernathy, A. Philip

Randolph, Benjamin Mays, and Martin Luther King Jr. But I'm also drawn to two other names: Rabbi Uri Miller and Rabbi Joachim Prinz, two Jewish Americans who lent their voices to the March. Prinz (of the American Jewish Congress) and Rabbi Abraham Joshua Heschel were close allies of Dr. King. They were part of a generation of Jewish Americans who fought alongside African Americans for our rights in a Black-Jewish alliance that dates back to the turn of the century.

Five years before the March on Washington, in 1958, Dr. King addressed the American Jewish Congress at a convention held at their sun-drenched Miami Beach headquarters. He asked the Jewish leaders and their allies from around the country to join his fight and reminded the audience of their shared history of slavery and persecution. "There are Hitlers loose in America today, both in high and low places," King said to the leaders at the American Jewish Congress Convention in his remarks. "This is a time for vigorous and positive action."

King's appeal to an alliance with Jewish leaders was a half century in the making. In 1908, the NAACP was formed in response to the Springfield Massacre, which targeted over one thousand Black people. American Jews such as Henry Moskowitz, Stephen Wise, Joel Elias Spingarn, Jacob Schiff, and Jacob Billikopf were among the organization's founders and supporters. Their involvement exemplified a shared commitment to civil rights and justice.

After the divisive 1896 Supreme Court decision in *Plessy v. Ferguson*, which upheld "separate but equal" and entrenched racial segregation, Jewish businessman and philanthropist Julius Rosenwald stepped in to fill the education gap for Black children. Rosenwald partnered with Booker T. Washington to open more than five thousand primary, secondary, and postsecondary schools for Black students. At one point, these schools educated one-third of Black children in the South.

Across the ocean, the pogroms and genocide of Jews in Eastern Europe that began in the 1930s were tragically linked to the racial oppression experienced by Black Americans. The infamous Nuremberg Laws, created by the Nazis in Germany, were modeled after the American system of Jim Crow. In fact, according to the Prussian Memorandum, the Nazis ultimately decided not to fully implement Jim Crow–style segregation, recognizing that, unlike Black Americans, Jews had a strong economic base that could initially resist such measures. Fittingly, when the United States entered World War II to fight Hitler and the Axis powers, Black men enlisted in record numbers to defeat tyranny abroad, even as they continued to fight for equality at home.

Black men like my grandfather enlisted to fight Hitler and end his genocide of Jewish people. Black GIs anointed the Double Victory Campaign—also called the Double V Campaign—which stood for victory over Nazism and fascism abroad and victory over racism at home. In May of 1945, an all-Black army unit, the 761st Tank

Battalion, liberated fifteen thousand people from the horrors of the Gunskirchen concentration camp in Austria. After the war, the alliance continued when Jewish Americans participated in the civil rights movement in large numbers.

Given this history of mutual support, it's no surprise that Jewish Americans became an integral part of Dr. King's coalition. Yet, King's vision of justice extended further, embracing South Asian and Latinx leaders as well. In 1959, he traveled to India to learn from activists who had worked alongside Gandhi to resist colonial oppression and white supremacy. Following the Montgomery Bus Boycott, King began corresponding with Latinx leader Cesar Chavez, exchanging ideas on advocating for economic justice.

Dr. King played a pivotal role in building an alliance between Black Americans and the Asian American Pacific Islander (AAPI) community. In 1963, Asian American civil rights activist Grace Lee Boggs organized a march for King in Detroit, where he gave an earlier version of the "I Have a Dream" speech. Boggs, inspired by King, went on to carry his legacy of nonviolent resistance until she passed away in 2015. Yuri Kochiyama, a Japanese American activist who was a leader in the Black Liberation movement, was also inspired by Dr. King and sent her son to participate in the Freedom Rides with King's ally John Lewis. Notably, Dr. King also stood with the AAPI community in protesting the Vietnam War, showing solidarity with leaders like Kochiyama and the Asian American Political Alliance.

Jewish civil rights leaders played a crucial role in the movement, actively participating in voter drives, campus protests, sit-ins, and marches throughout the 1950s and 1960s. Tragically, two Jewish individuals, Michael Schwerner and Andrew Goodman—alongside African American activist James Chaney—were murdered by the KKK while working to register voters in Mississippi.

In 1958, Stanley Levinson, a Jewish attorney, raised funds for the Montgomery Bus Boycott. Levinson served as King's personal accountant and advisor for the remainder of King's life. Rabbi Joachim Prinz and Rabbi Abraham Joshua Heschel were also key figures, offering counsel and support to King throughout the 1960s. At the March on Washington, Rabbi Prinz delivered a stirring speech that resonated with King's call for action made at the American Jewish Congress Convention five years earlier. Prinz, reflecting on his experiences as a rabbi in Berlin under the Hitler regime, proclaimed, "The most important thing I learned under those tragic circumstances was that bigotry and hatred are not the most urgent problems. The most urgent, the most disgraceful, the most shameful, and the most tragic problem is silence." Prinz made this declaration moments before King delivered his iconic "I Have a Dream" speech.

The drafting of the Civil Rights Act of 1964 occurred within the walls of the American Jewish Congress building in Washington, DC, which donated space to civil rights activists. However, after the civil rights movement, the battle for Black Americans shifted from civil rights to economic rights. The allyship of Jewish Americans stands as one of the most powerful bonds and partnerships in history. Today there is much more work for us to do together for the benefit of both our communities.

My friend Robert Kraft, the New England Patriots owner, embodies an ally. He and I are founding members of the REFORM Alliance, an organization dedicated to addressing criminal justice reform in the United States. With the US having one of the highest incarceration rates in the world and a disproportionate number of those incarcerated being people of color, particularly those who have been over-sentenced or denied parole, the REFORM Alliance has a critical mission. Mr. Kraft stepped up to help me overcome this challenge disproportionately affecting African Americans. The REFORM Alliance focuses on transforming probation and parole practices, advocating for fair sentencing, and seeking to reduce the number of individuals under community supervision. Kraft is standing with the African American community as we work to reshape our nation's approach to criminal justice for the better.

Another friend of mine who has been a quintessential ally is former New York City mayor Michael Bloomberg. He has donated to HBCUs and medical schools. These investments will pay dividends by helping reduce systemic disparities in educational attainment and healthcare. His actions serve as a call to action for others in positions of influence to follow suit, ensuring that the quest for justice and equality is not just a dream but a tangible reality for all.

I also want to highlight the bipartisan effort of two public servants: Senator Chuck Schumer and Secretary Steve Mnuchin. I worked with them to ensure African American businesses and communities received aid during the pandemic. When the COVID-19 pandemic hit, communities of color were reeling, and it was abundantly clear that among the most brutally hit were Black-owned businesses. Due to low bank branch density in African American communities, Black entrepreneurs were not getting access to Paycheck Protection Program (PPP) loans at the same rate as other business owners. With Steve Mnuchin, the former US secretary of the treasury, and Chuck Schumer, the Senate Majority Leader, we secured essential funding for the African American community through access to PPP loans. Efforts like those of Senator Schumer, Secretary Mnuchin, and Mr. Kraft are examples of the type of allyship that continues the tradition of fraternity in justice between Black people and the American Jewish community. These are just some examples of the type of impactful work that can be accomplished through allyship.

My grandfather and thousands of other African Americans fought Hitler during World War II; thirty years later, my mother and father, with me in tow, watched on the National Mall as Jewish allies stood with Dr. King in the civil rights movement. History serves as a reminder that African Americans must stand with Jewish Americans as we ask them to stand with us. We must reject ideas of anti-Semitism at home and abroad and raise our voices for our brothers and sisters when they need allyship.

As I call my brothers and sisters back into the struggle for justice for African Americans, I think of the famous photo of Dr. King leading the March across the Edmund Pettus Bridge in Selma in 1965. In it, a young Dr. King is surrounded by Black luminaries and activists, but to his right is Rabbi Joshua Hershel, who has his signature long, curly white beard and thick-framed black glasses. The men wore Hawaiian leis with dark suits, a symbol of allyship with the AAPI community. I revisit that photo as a reminder of what our communities working together have accomplished. It symbolizes hope, unity, and the indomitable spirit of those who dare to dream of a better world. As we confront the challenges of today, let us stand together once more, ready to face the unique trials with renewed determination. We can build a future anchored in justice, equality, and the unbreakable ties that define our shared journey.

Dr. King's example of allyship has provided me with a pathway for thinking about the role of partners and advocates in all aspects of my life—business, philanthropy, leadership—and the critical process of building and deepening relationships. His demonstration of the power of having people from different walks of life singing from the same hymnal to achieve a desired outcome is genuinely inspiring.

Reflecting on Dr. King's legacy, it's clear that anyone can benefit from forging thoughtful alliances. To that end, we cannot overlook the importance of allies in advancing racial equity, as we saw in the George Floyd movement, a movement of intersectional justice we now need to reinvigorate.

How can you bring together communities to foster dialogue and create lasting change? Dr. King exemplified how strategic alliances can drive systemic change for marginalized groups. I encourage clergy leaders to take the lead in creating spaces for connection—just as I helped lead a joint Hanukkah-Kwanzaa celebration in 2022 to bridge the gap between the Black and Jewish communities. Whether you attend a church, mosque, temple, or synagogue, urge your clergy leaders to initiate these kinds of efforts, turning them into ongoing activities that foster unity and collective action.

Smith with (left to right) Judy Forte, Bernice A. King, his aunt Linda Wilson, and Angela Christine Farris Watkins in the King family home in Atlanta, which was purchased by Smith and transferred to the National Park Foundation for preservation.

Dr. King leads civil rights marchers in Montgomery, Alabama. Also pictured are John Lewis of the Student Nonviolent Coordinating Committee (second from left), Reverend Ralph Abernathy (third from left), Dr. Ralph Bunche (fifth from left), Mrs. King (next to Dr. King), and Reverend Hosea Williams (carrying a little girl). March 25, 1965.

Bettman

Man in the Arena

"Letter from Birmingham City Jail"

My dear Fellow Clergymen,

While confined here in the Birmingham city jail, I came across your recent statement calling our present activities "unwise and untimely." Seldom, if ever, do I pause to answer criticism of my work and ideas. If I sought to answer all of the criticisms that cross my desk, my secretaries would be engaged in little else in the course of the day, and I would have no time for constructive work. But since I feel that you are men of genuine goodwill and your criticisms are sincerely set forth, I would like to answer your statement in what I hope will be patient and reasonable terms.

I think I should give the reason for my being in Birmingham, since you have been influenced by the argument of "outsiders coming in." I have the honor of serving as president of the Southern Christian Leadership Conference, an organization operating in every Southern state, with headquarters in Atlanta, Georgia. We have some eighty-five affiliate organizations all across the South—one being the Alabama Christian Movement for Human Rights. Whenever necessary and possible we share staff, educational, and financial resources with our affiliates. Several months ago our local affiliate here in Birmingham invited us to be on call to engage in a nonviolent direct-action program if such were deemed necessary. We readily consented and when the hour came we lived up to our promises. So I am here, along with several members of my staff, because we were invited here. I am here because I have basic organizational ties here.

Beyond this, I am in Birmingham because injustice is here. Just as the eighth-century prophets left their little villages and carried their "thus saith the Lord" far beyond the boundaries of their hometowns; and just as the Apostle Paul left his little village of Tarsus and carried the gospel of Jesus Christ to the far corners of the Greco-Roman world, I too am compelled to carry the gospel of freedom beyond my particular hometown. Like Paul, I must constantly respond to the Macedonian call for aid.

Moreover, I am cognizant of the interrelatedness of all communities and states. I cannot sit idly by in Atlanta and not be concerned about what happens in Birmingham. Injustice anywhere is a threat to justice everywhere. We are caught in an inescapable network of mutuality, tied in a single garment of destiny. Whatever affects one directly affects all indirectly. Never again can we afford to live with the narrow, provincial "outside agitator" idea. Anyone who lives inside the United States can never be considered an outsider anywhere in this country.

You deplore the demonstrations that are presently taking place in Birmingham. But I am sorry that your statement did not express a similar concern for the conditions that brought the demonstrations into being. I am sure that each of you would want to go beyond the superficial social analyst who looks merely at effects and does not grapple with underlying causes. I would not hesitate to say that it is unfortunate that so-called demonstrations are taking place in Birmingham at this time, but I would say in more emphatic terms that it is even more unfortunate that the white power structure of this city left the Negro community with no other alternative.

In any nonviolent campaign there are four basic steps: (1) collection of the facts to determine whether injustices are alive, (2) negotiation, (3) self-purification, and (4) direct action. We have gone through all of these steps in Birmingham. There can be no gainsaying of the fact that racial injustice engulfs this community.

Birmingham is probably the most thoroughly segregated city in the United States. Its ugly record of brutality is known in every section of this country. Its unjust treatment of Negroes in the courts is a notorious reality. There have been more unsolved bombings of Negro homes and churches in Birmingham than any city in this nation. These are the hard, brutal, and unbelievable facts. On the basis of these conditions, Negro leaders sought to negotiate with the city fathers. But the political leaders consistently refused to engage in good-faith negotiation.

Then came the opportunity last September to talk with some of the leaders of the economic community. In these negotiating sessions certain promises were made by the merchants—such as the promise to remove the humiliating racial signs from the stores. On the basis of these promises Rev. Shuttlesworth and the leaders of the Alabama Christian Movement for Human Rights agreed to call a moratorium on any type of demonstrations. As the weeks and months unfolded we realized that we were the victims of a broken promise. The signs remained. Like so many experiences of the past we were confronted with blasted hopes, and the dark shadow of a deep disappointment settled upon us. So we had no alternative except that of preparing for direct action, whereby we would present our very bodies as a means of laying our case before the conscience of the local and the national community. We were not unmindful of the difficulties involved. So we decided to go through a process of self-purification. We started having workshops on nonviolence and repeatedly asked ourselves the questions, "Are you able to accept blows without retaliating?" "Are you able to endure the ordeals of jail?" We decided to set our direct-action program around the Easter season, realizing that with the exception of Christmas, this was the largest shopping period of the year. Knowing that a strong economic withdrawal program would be the by-product of direct action, we felt that this was the best time to bring pressure on the merchants for the needed changes. Then it occurred to us that the March election was ahead and so we speedily decided to postpone action until after election day. When we discovered that Mr. Connor was in the run-off, we decided again to postpone action so that the demonstrations could not be used to cloud the issues. At this time we agreed to begin our nonviolent witness the day after the runoff.

This reveals that we did not move irresponsibly into direct action. We too wanted to see Mr. Connor defeated; so we went through postponement after postponement to aid in this community need. After this we felt that direct action could be delayed no longer.

You may well ask, "Why direct action? Why sit-ins, marches, etc.? Isn't negotiation a better path?" You are exactly right in your call for negotiation. Indeed, this is the purpose of direct action. Nonviolent direct action seeks to create such a crisis and establish such creative tension that a community that has constantly refused to negotiate is forced to confront the issue. It seeks so to dramatize the issue that it can no longer be ignored. I just referred to the creation of tension as a part of the work of the nonviolent resister. This may sound rather shocking. But I must confess that I am not afraid of the word *tension*. I have earnestly worked and preached against violent tension, but there is a type of constructive nonviolent tension that is necessary for growth. Just as Socrates felt that it was necessary to create a tension in the mind so that individuals could rise from the bondage of myths and half-truths to the unfettered realm of creative analysis and objective appraisal, we must see the need of having nonviolent gadflies to create the kind of tension in society that will help men rise from the dark depths of prejudice and racism to the majestic heights of understanding and brotherhood. So the purpose of the direct action is to create a situation so crisis-packed that it will inevitably open the door to negotiation. We, therefore, concur with you in your call for negotiation. Too long has our beloved Southland been bogged down in the tragic attempt to live in monologue rather than dialogue.

One of the basic points in your statement is that our acts are untimely. Some have asked, "Why didn't you give the new administration time to act?" The only answer that I can give to this inquiry is that the new administration must be prodded about as much as the outgoing one before it acts. We will be sadly mistaken if we feel that the election of Mr. Boutwell will bring the millennium to Birmingham. While Mr. Boutwell is much more articulate and gentle than Mr. Connor, they are both segregationists, dedicated to the task of maintaining the status quo. The hope I see in Mr. Boutwell is that he will be reasonable enough to see the futility of massive resistance to desegregation. But he will not see this without pressure from the devotees of civil rights. My friends, I must say to you that we have not made a single gain in civil rights without determined legal and nonviolent pressure. History is the long and tragic story of the fact that privileged groups seldom give up their privileges voluntarily. Individuals may see the moral light and voluntarily give up their unjust posture; but as Reinhold Niebuhr has reminded us, groups are more immoral than individuals.

We know through painful experience that freedom is never voluntarily given by the oppressor; it must be demanded by the oppressed. Frankly, I have never yet engaged in a direct-action movement that was "well-timed," according to the timetable of those who have not suffered unduly from the disease of segregation. For years now I have heard the word "Wait!" It rings in the ear of every Negro with a piercing familiarity. This "Wait" has almost always meant "Never." It has been a tranquilizing thalidomide, relieving the emotional stress for a moment, only to give birth to an ill-formed infant of frustration. We must come to see with the distinguished jurist of yesterday that "justice too long delayed is justice denied." We have waited for more than 340 years for our constitutional and God-given rights. The nations of Asia and Africa are moving with jetlike speed toward the goal of political independence, and we still creep at horse and buggy pace toward the gaining of a cup of coffee at a lunch counter. I guess it is easy for those who have never felt the stinging darts of segregation to say, "Wait." But when you have seen vicious mobs lynch your mothers and fathers at will and drown your sisters and brothers at whim; when you have seen hate-filled policemen curse, kick, brutalize, and even kill your Black brothers and sisters with impunity; when you see the vast majority of your twenty million Negro brothers smothering in an airtight cage of poverty in the midst of an affluent society; when you suddenly find your tongue twisted and your speech stammering as you seek to explain to your six-year-old daughter why she can't go to the public amusement park that has just been advertised on television, and see tears welling up in her eyes when she is told that Funtown is closed to colored children, and see the depressing clouds of inferiority beginning to form in her little mental sky, and see her begin to distort her little personality by unconsciously developing a bitterness toward white people; when you have to concoct an answer for a five-year-old son asking in agonizing pathos, "Daddy, why do white people treat colored people so mean?"; when you take a cross-country drive and find it necessary to sleep night after night in the uncomfortable corners of your automobile because no motel will accept you; when you are humiliated day in and day out by nagging signs reading "white" and "colored"; when your first name becomes "nigger" and your middle name becomes "boy" (however old you are) and your last name becomes "John," and when your wife and mother are never given the respected title "Mrs."; when you are harried by day and haunted by night by the fact that you are a Negro, living constantly at tiptoe stance never quite knowing what to expect next, and plagued with inner fears and outer resentments; when you are forever fighting a degenerating sense of "nobodiness"; then you will understand why we find it difficult to wait. There comes a time when the cup of endurance runs over, and men are no longer willing to be plunged into an abyss of injustice where they experience the blackness of corroding despair. I hope, sirs, you can understand our legitimate and unavoidable impatience.

You express a great deal of anxiety over our willingness to break laws. This is certainly a legitimate concern. Since we so diligently urge people to obey the Supreme Court's decision of 1954 outlawing segregation in the public schools, it is rather strange and paradoxical to find us consciously breaking laws. One may well ask, "How can you advocate breaking some laws and obeying others?" The answer is found in the fact that there are two types of laws: There are *just* and there are *unjust* laws. I would agree with Saint Augustine that "an unjust law is no law at all."

Now what is the difference between the two? How does one determine when a law is just or unjust? A just law is a man-made code that squares with the moral law or the law of God. An unjust law is a code that is out of harmony with the moral law. To put it in the terms of

Saint Thomas Aquinas, an unjust law is a human law that is not rooted in eternal and natural law. Any law that uplifts human personality is just. Any law that degrades human personality is unjust. All segregation statutes are unjust because segregation distorts the soul and damages the personality. It gives the segregator a false sense of superiority, and the segregated a false sense of inferiority. To use the words of Martin Buber, the great Jewish philosopher, segregation substitutes an "I-it" relationship for the "I-thou" relationship, and ends up relegating persons to the status of things. So segregation is not only politically, economically, and sociologically unsound, but it is morally wrong and sinful. Paul Tillich has said that sin is separation. Isn't segregation an existential expression of man's tragic separation, an expression of his awful estrangement, his terrible sinfulness? So I can urge men to disobey segregation ordinances because they are morally wrong.

Let us turn to a more concrete example of just and unjust laws. An unjust law is a code that a majority inflicts on a minority that is not binding on itself. This is difference made legal. On the other hand a just law is a code that a majority compels a minority to follow that it is willing to follow itself. This is sameness made legal.

Let me give another explanation. An unjust law is a code inflicted upon a minority which that minority had no part in enacting or creating because they did not have the unhampered right to vote. Who can say that the legislature of Alabama which set up the segregation laws was democratically elected? Throughout the state of Alabama all types of conniving methods are used to prevent Negroes from becoming registered voters, and there are some counties without a single Negro registered to vote despite the fact that the Negro constitutes a majority of the population. Can any law set up in such a state be considered democratically structured?

These are just a few examples of unjust and just laws. There are some instances when a law is just on its face and unjust in its application. For instance, I was arrested Friday on a charge of parading without a permit. Now there is nothing wrong with an ordinance which requires a permit for a parade, but when the ordinance is used to preserve segregation and to deny citizens the First Amendment privilege of peaceful assembly and peaceful protest, then it becomes unjust.

I hope you can see the distinction I am trying to point out. In no sense do I advocate evading or defying the law as the rabid segregationist would do. That would lead to anarchy. One who breaks an unjust law must do it *openly*, *lovingly* (not hatefully as the white mothers did in New Orleans when they were seen on television screaming, "Nigger, nigger, nigger"), and with a willingness to accept the penalty. I submit that an individual who breaks a law that conscience tells him is unjust, and willingly accepts the penalty by staying in jail to arouse the conscience of the community over its injustice, is in reality expressing the very highest respect for law.

Of course, there is nothing new about this kind of civil disobedi-ence. It was seen sublimely in the refusal of Shadrach, Meshach, and Abednego to obey the laws of Nebuchadnezzar because a higher moral law was involved. It was practiced superbly by the early Christians who were willing to face hungry lions and the excruciating pain of chopping blocks before submitting to certain unjust laws of the Roman Empire. To a degree academic freedom is a reality today because Socrates prac-ticed civil disobedience.

We can never forget that everything Hitler did in Germany was "le-gal" and everything the Hungarian freedom fighters did in Hungary was "illegal." It was "illegal" to aid and comfort a Jew in Hitler's Germany. But I am sure that if I had lived in Germany during that time I would have aided and comforted my Jewish brothers even though it was il-legal. If I lived in a Communist country today where certain principles dear to the Christian faith are suppressed, I believe I would openly ad-vocate disobeying these anti-religious laws. I must make two honest confessions to you, my Christian and Jewish brothers. First, I must con-fess that over the last few years I have been gravely disappointed with the white moderate. I have almost reached the regrettable conclusion that the Negro's great stumbling block in the stride toward freedom is not the White Citizen's Counciler or the Ku Klux Klanner, but the white moderate who is more devoted to "order" than to justice; who prefers a negative peace which is the absence of tension to a positive peace which is the presence of justice; who constantly says, "I agree with you in the goal you seek, but I cannot agree with your methods of direct action"; who paternalistically feels he can set the timetable for another man's freedom; who lives by the myth of time and who constantly advises the Negro to wait until a "more convenient season." Shallow understanding from people of goodwill is more frustrating than absolute misunderstanding from people of ill will. Lukewarm acceptance is much more bewildering than outright rejection.

I had hoped that the white moderate would understand that law and order exist for the purpose of establishing justice, and that when they fail to do this they become dangerously structured dams that block the flow of social progress. I had hoped that the white moderate would understand that the present tension in the South is merely a necessary phase of the transition from an obnoxious negative peace, where the Negro passively accepted his unjust plight, to a substance-filled positive peace, where all men will respect the dignity and worth of human personality. Actually, we who engage in nonviolent direct action are not the creators of tension. We merely bring to the surface the hidden tension that is already alive. We bring it out in the open where it can be seen and dealt with. Like a boil that can never be cured as long as it is covered up but must be opened, with all its pus-flowing ugliness, to the natural medicines of air and light, injustice must likewise be exposed, with all of the tension its exposing creates, to the light of human conscience and the air of national opinion before it can be cured.

In your statement you asserted that our actions, even though peaceful, must be condemned because they precipitate violence. But can this assertion be logically made? Isn't this like condemning the robbed man because his possession of money precipitated the evil act of robbery? Isn't this like condemning Socrates because his unswerving commitment to truth and his philosophical delvings precipitated the misguided popular mind to make him drink the hemlock? Isn't this like condemning Jesus because his unique God-consciousness and never-ceasing devotion to his will precipitated the evil act of crucifixion? We must come to see, as federal courts have consistently affirmed, that it is immoral to urge an individual to withdraw his efforts to gain his basic constitutional rights because the quest precipitates violence. Society must protect the robbed and punish the robber.

I had also hoped that the white moderate would reject the myth of time. I received a letter this morning from a white brother in Texas which said: "All Christians know that the colored people will receive equal rights eventually, but it is possible that you are in too great of a religious hurry. It has taken Christianity almost two thousand years to accomplish what it has. The teachings of Christ take time to come to earth." All that is said here grows out of a tragic misconception of time. It is the strangely irrational notion that there is something in the very flow of time that will inevitably cure all ills. Actually time is neutral. It can be used either destructively or constructively. I am coming to feel that the people of ill will have used time much more effectively than the people of good will. We will have to repent in this generation not merely for the vitriolic words and actions of the bad people, but for the appalling silence of the good people. We must come to see that human progress never rolls in on wheels of inevitability. It comes through the tireless efforts and persistent work of men willing to be coworkers with God, and without this hard work time itself becomes an ally of the forces of social stagnation. We must use time creatively, and forever realize that the time is always ripe to do right. Now is the time to make real the promise of democracy, and transform our pending national elegy into a creative psalm of brotherhood. Now is the time to lift our national policy from the quicksand of racial injustice to the solid rock of human dignity.

You spoke of our activity in Birmingham as extreme. At first I was rather disappointed that fellow clergymen would see my nonviolent efforts as those of the extremist. I started thinking about the fact that I stand in the middle of two opposing forces in the Negro community. One is a force of complacency made up of Negroes who, as a result of long years of oppression, have been so completely drained of self-respect and a sense of "somebodiness" that they have adjusted to segregation, and, of a few Negroes in the middle class who, because of a degree of academic and economic security, and because at points they profit by segregation, have unconsciously become insensitive to the problems of the masses. The other force is one of bitterness and hatred, and comes perilously close to advocating violence. It is expressed in the various Black nationalist groups that are springing up all over the nation, the largest and best known being Elijah Muhammad's Muslim movement. This movement is nourished by the contemporary frustration over the continued existence of racial discrimination. It is made up of people who have lost faith in America, who have absolutely repudiated Christianity, and who have concluded that the white man is an incurable "devil." I have tried to stand between these two forces, saying that we need not follow the "do-nothingism" of the complacent or the hatred and despair of the Black nationalist. There is the more excellent way of love and nonviolent protest. I'm grateful to God that, through the Negro church, the dimension of nonviolence entered our struggle. If this philosophy had not emerged, I am convinced that by now many streets of the South would be flowing with floods of blood. And I am further convinced that if our white brothers dismiss as "rabble-rousers" and "outside agitators" those of us who are working through the channels of nonviolent direct action and refuse to support our nonviolent efforts, millions of Negroes, out of frustration and despair, will seek solace and security in Black nationalist ideologies, a development that will lead inevitably to a frightening racial nightmare.

Oppressed people cannot remain oppressed forever. The urge for freedom will eventually come. This is what happened to the American Negro. Something within has reminded him of his birthright of freedom; something without has reminded him that he can gain it. Consciously and unconsciously, he has been swept in by what the Germans call the *Zeitgeist*, and with his Black brothers of Africa, and his brown and yellow brothers of Asia, South America, and the Caribbean, he is moving with a sense of cosmic urgency toward the promised land of racial justice. Recognizing this vital urge that has engulfed the Negro community, one should readily understand public demonstrations. The Negro has many pent-up resentments and latent frustrations. He has to get them out. So let him march sometime; let him have his prayer pilgrimages to the city hall; understand why he must have sit-ins and freedom rides. If his repressed emotions do not come out in these nonviolent ways, they will come out in ominous expressions of violence. This is not a threat; it is a fact of history. So I have not said to my people, "Get rid of your discontent." But I have tried to say that this normal and healthy discontent can be channelized through the creative outlet of nonviolent direct action. Now this approach is being dismissed as extremist. I must admit that I was initially disappointed in being so categorized.

But as I continued to think about the matter I gradually gained a bit of satisfaction from being considered an extremist. Was not Jesus an extremist in love—"Love your enemies, bless them that curse you, pray for them that despitefully use you." Was not Amos an extrem- ist for justice—"Let justice roll down like waters and righteousness like a mighty stream." Was not Paul an extremist for the gospel of Jesus Christ—"I bear in my body the marks of the Lord Jesus." Was not Mar- tin Luther an extremist—"Here I stand; I cannot do otherwise, so help me God." Was not John Bunyan an extremist—"I will stay in jail to the end of my days before I make a butchery of my conscience." Was not Abraham Lincoln an extremist—"This nation cannot survive half slave and half free." Was not Thomas Jefferson an extremist—"We hold these truths to be self-evident, that all men are created equal." So the question is not whether we will be extremist but what kind of extremist will we be? Will we be extremists for hate or will we be extremists for love? Will we be extremists for the preservation of injustice—or will we be extremists for the cause of justice? In that dramatic scene on Cal- vary's hill, three men were crucified. We must not forget that all three were crucified for the same crime—the crime of extremism. Two were extremists for immorality, and thusly fell below their environment. The other, Jesus Christ, was an extremist for love, truth, and goodness, and thereby rose above his environment. So, after all, maybe the South, the nation, and the world are in dire need of creative extremists.

I had hoped that the white moderate would see this. Maybe I was too optimistic. Maybe I expected too much. I guess I should have real- ized that few members of a race that has oppressed another race can understand or appreciate the deep groans and passionate yearnings of those that have been oppressed and still fewer have the vision to see that injustice must be rooted out by strong, persistent, and determined action. I am thankful, however, that some of our white brothers have grasped the meaning of this social revolution and committed themselves to it. They are still all too small in quantity, but they are big in quality. Some like as Ralph McGill, Lillian Smith, Harry Golden, and James Dabbs have written about our struggle in eloquent, prophetic, and understanding terms. Others have marched with us down nameless streets of the South. They have languished in filthy, roach-infested jails, suffering the abuse and brutality of angry policemen who see them as "dirty nigger-lovers." They, unlike so many of their moderate brothers and sisters, have recognized the urgency of the moment and sensed the need for powerful "action" antidotes to combat the disease of segregation.

Let me rush on to mention my other major disappointment. I have been so greatly disappointed with the white church and its leadership. Of course, there are some notable exceptions. I am not unmindful of the fact that each of you has taken some significant stands on this issue. I commend you, Reverend Stallings, for your Christian stance on this past Sunday, in welcoming Negroes to your worship service on a non-segregated basis. I commend the Catholic leaders of this state for integrating Spring Hill College several years ago.

But despite these notable exceptions I must honestly reiterate that

I have been disappointed with the church. I do not say that as one of those negative critics who can always find something wrong with the church. I say this as a minister of the gospel, who loves the church; who was nurtured in its bosom; who has been sustained by its spiritual blessings and who will remain true to it as long as the cord of life shall lengthen.

I had the strange feeling when I was suddenly catapulted into the leadership of the bus protest in Montgomery several years ago that we would have the support of the white church. I felt that the white ministers, priests, and rabbis of the South would be some of our strongest allies. Instead, some have been outright opponents, refusing to understand the freedom movement and misrepresenting its leaders; all too many others have been more cautious than courageous and have remained silent behind the anesthetizing security of the stained-glass windows.

In spite of my shattered dreams of the past, I came to Birmingham with the hope that the white religious leadership of this community would see the justice of our cause, and with deep moral concern, serve as the channel through which our just grievances would get to the power structure. I had hoped that each of you would understand. But again I have been disappointed. I have heard numerous religious leaders of the South call upon their worshipers to comply with a desegregation decision because it is the *law*, but I have longed to hear white ministers say, "Follow this decree because integration is morally *right* and the Negro is your brother." In the midst of blatant injustices inflicted upon the Negro, I have watched white churches stand on the sideline and merely mouth pious irrelevancies and sanctimonious trivialities. In the midst of a mighty struggle to rid our nation of racial and economic injustice, I have heard so many ministers say, "Those are social issues with which the gospel has no real concern," and I have watched so many churches commit themselves to a completely otherworldly religion which made a strange distinction between body and soul, the sacred and the secular.

So here we are moving toward the exit of the twentieth century with a religious community largely adjusted to the status quo, standing as a taillight behind other community agencies rather than a headlight leading men to higher levels of justice.

I have traveled the length and breadth of Alabama, Mississippi, and all the other Southern states. On sweltering summer days and crisp autumn mornings I have looked at her beautiful churches with their lofty spires pointing heavenward. I have beheld the impressive outlay of her massive religious education buildings. Over and over again I have found myself asking: "What kind of people worship here? Who is their God? Where were their voices when the lips of Governor Barnett dripped with words of interposition and nullification? Where were they when Governor Wallace gave a clarion call for defiance and hatred? Where were their voices of support when tired, bruised, and weary Negro men and women decided to rise from the dark dungeons of complacency to the bright hills of creative protest?"

Yes, these questions are still in my mind. In deep disappointment, I have wept over the laxity of the church. But be assured that my tears have been tears of love. There can be no deep disappointment where there is not deep love. Yes, I love the church; I love her sacred walls. How could I do otherwise? I am in the rather unique position of being the son, the grandson, and the great-grandson of preachers. Yes, I see the church as the body of Christ. But, oh! How we have blemished and scarred that body through social neglect and through fear of being nonconformists.

There was a time when the church was very powerful. It was during that period when the early Christians rejoiced when they were deemed worthy to suffer for what they believed. In those days the church was not merely a thermometer that recorded the ideas and principles of popular opinion; it was a thermostat that transformed the mores of society. Whenever the early Christians entered a town, the power structure got disturbed and immediately sought to convict them for being "disturbers of the peace" and "outside agitators." But they went on with the conviction that they were "a colony of heaven," and had to obey God rather than man. They were small in number but big in commitment. They were too God-intoxicated to be "astronomically intimidated." They brought an end to such ancient evils as infanticide and gladiatorial contests.

Things are different now. The contemporary church is often a weak, ineffectual voice with an uncertain sound. It is so often the arch supporter of the status quo. Far from being disturbed by the presence of the church, the power structure of the average community is consoled by the church's silent and often vocal sanction of things as they are.

But the judgment of God is upon the church as never before. If the church of today does not recapture the sacrificial spirit of the early church, it will lose its authentic ring, forfeit the loyalty of millions, and be dismissed as an irrelevant social club with no meaning for the twentieth century. I am meeting young people every day whose disappointment with the church has risen to outright disgust.

Maybe again I have been too optimistic. Is organized religion too inextricably bound to the status quo to save our nation and the world? Maybe I must turn my faith to the inner spiritual church, the church within the church, as the true *ecclesia* and the hope of the world. But again I am thankful to God that some noble souls from the ranks of organized religion have broken loose from the paralyzing chains of conformity and joined us as active partners in the struggle for freedom. They have left their secure congregations and walked the streets of Albany, Georgia, with us. They have gone through the highways of the South on tortuous rides for freedom. Yes, they have gone to jail with us. Some have been kicked out of their churches, and lost the support of their bishops and fellow ministers. But they have gone with the faith that right defeated is stronger than evil triumphant. These men have been the leaven in the lump of the race. Their witness has been the spiritual salt that has preserved the true meaning of the gospel in these troubled times. They have carved a tunnel of hope through the dark mountain of disappointment.

I hope the church as a whole will meet the challenge of this decisive hour. But even if the church does not come to the aid of justice, I have no despair about the future. I have no fear about the outcome of our struggle in Birmingham, even if our motives are presently misunderstood. We will reach the goal of freedom in Birmingham and all over the nation, because the goal of America is freedom. Abused and scorned though we may be, our destiny is tied up with the destiny of America. Before the Pilgrims landed at Plymouth we were here. Before the pen of Jefferson etched across the pages of history the majestic words of the Declaration of Independence, we were here. For more than two centuries our foreparents labored in this country without wages; they made cotton king; and they built the homes of their masters in the midst of brtual injustice and shameful humiliation—and yet out of a bottomless vitality they continued to thrive and develop. If the inexpressible cruelties of slavery could not stop us, the opposition we now face will surely fail. We will win our freedom because the sacred heritage of our nation and the eternal will of God are embodied in our echoing demands.

I must close now. But before closing I am impelled to mention one other point in your statement that troubled me profoundly. You warmly commended the Birmingham police force for keeping "order" and "preventing violence." I don't believe you would have so warmly commended the police force if you had seen its angry, violent dogs literally biting six unarmed, nonviolent Negroes. I don't believe you would so quickly commend the policemen if you would observe their ugly and inhumane treatment of Negroes here in the city jail; if you would watch them push and curse old Negro women and young Negro girls; if you would see them slap and kick old Negro men and young boys; if you would observe them, as they did on two occasions, refuse to give us food because we wanted to sing our grace together. I'm sorry that I can't join you in your praise for the police department.

It is true that they have been rather disciplined in their public handling of the demonstrators. In this sense they have been rather publicly "nonviolent." But for what purpose? To preserve the evil system of segregation. Over the last few years I have consistently preached that nonviolence demands that the means we use must be as pure as the ends we seek. So I have tried to make it clear that it is wrong to use immoral means to attain moral ends. But now I must affirm that it is just as wrong, or even more so, to use moral means to preserve immoral ends. Maybe Mr. Connor and his policemen have been rather publicly nonviolent, as Chief Pritchett was in Albany, Georgia, but they have used the moral means of nonviolence to maintain the immoral end of flagrant racial injustice. T. S. Eliot has said that there is no greater treason than to do the right deed for the wrong reason.

I wish you had commended the Negro sit-inners and demonstrators of Birmingham for their sublime courage, their willingness to suffer, and their amazing discipline in the midst of the most inhuman provocation. One day the South will recognize its real heroes. They will be the James Merediths, courageously and with a majestic sense of purpose facing jeering and hostile mobs and the agonizing loneliness that character-izes the life of the pioneer. They will be old, oppressed, battered Negro women, symbolized in a seventy-two-year-old woman of Montgom-ery, Alabama, who rose up with a sense of dignity and with her people decided not to ride the segregated buses, and responded to one who inquired about her tiredness with ungrammatical profundity: "My feet is tired, but my soul is rested." They will be the young high school and college students, young ministers of the gospel and a host of their el-ders courageously and nonviolently sitting-in at lunch counters and will-ingly going to jail for consciences' sake. One day the South will know that when these disinherited children of God sat down at lunch count-ers they were in reality standing up for the best in the American dream and the most sacred values in our Judeo-Christian heritage, and thusly, carrying our whole nation back to those great wells of democracy which were dug deep by the Founding Fathers in the formulation of the Con-stitution and the Declaration of Independence.

Never before have I written a letter this long (or should I say a book?). I'm afraid that it is much too long to take your precious time. I can assure you that it would have been much shorter if I had been writing from a comfortable desk, but what else is there to do when you are alone for days in the dull monotony of a narrow jail cell other than write long letters, think strange thoughts, and pray long prayers?

If I have said anything in this letter that is an overstatement of the truth and is indicative of an unreasonable impatience, I beg you to forgive me. If I have said anything in this letter that is an understatement of the truth and is indicative of my having a patience that makes me patient with anything less than brotherhood, I beg God to forgive me.

I hope this letter finds you strong in the faith. I also hope that circumstances will soon make it possible for me to meet each of you, not as an integrationist or a civil rights leader, but as a fellow clergyman and a Christian brother. Let us all hope that the dark clouds of racial prejudice will soon pass away and the deep fog of misunderstanding will be lifted from our fear-drenched communities and in some not-too-distant tomorrow the radiant stars of love and brotherhood will shine over our great nation with all of their scintillating beauty.

Yours for the cause of Peace and Brotherhood,

Martin Luther King Jr.

—Dr. Martin Luther King Jr.
April 16, 1963, Birmingham, Alabama

In "Letter from Birmingham City Jail," Dr. King wrote to his critics who claimed that the Atlanta leader was overstepping by traveling to Alabama to desegregate Birmingham. His iconic words in the letter—"Injustice anywhere is a threat to justice everywhere"—not only answers his detractors but serves as a reminder that we must act for the greater good even when it is uncomfortable. His example shows all of us the power of stepping up when our time comes.

In the 1990s, I began working at Goldman Sachs. I remember having my first meetings with pension fund groups and their managers and boards. I would ride the elevator up to the top floors of tall office buildings and make my way into large boardrooms with marble and glass tables to meet with decision-makers for pension funds. When I looked around the table, I would see friendly-enough faces in pressed suits and neatly knotted ties, but I noticed something else: No one in those rooms looked like me.

The pension fund management groups seated across from me were predominantly white, but they were in charge of investing the pension contributions of thousands of minority workers. It didn't sit right with me. I couldn't help but think of my mom and dad, sitting around the kitchen table in our family home in northeast Denver when I was a kid, balancing their checkbooks and sending off their dues and pension contributions to the teachers' union every month.

While union workers who contribute to pensions are about one-third minorities, only about 1.4 percent of the people who manage their funds are minorities. This disconnect can be a driver of racial disparity. Less diverse management groups are less likely to invest in businesses owned by people of color or companies that operate in communities of color. There's also a dark side to this issue: Some funds have been invested in private prisons, payday lenders, or real estate developers that push people out of their own communities.

Sitting in that boardroom looking out the top-floor windows, I realized that there was a role I needed to play. I believe it's essential that pension funds are managed by groups that look like the constituents of the union halls to which the funds belong. As the only African American in those executive suites, I realized it was up to folks like me to be the voice of those who weren't in the room. To step up and be what Theodore Roosevelt called "the man in the arena."

In 1901, President Theodore Roosevelt gave a speech at Sorbonne University in Paris. In his speech, he encouraged people to get involved in civic, community, and political action to better the world and to disregard the criticism of those who remained on the sidelines. "The credit belongs to the man who is actually in the arena, whose face is marred by dust and sweat and blood; who strives valiantly; who errs, who comes short . . . but who . . . spends himself in a worthy cause," Roosevelt said. Roosevelt's concept of getting in the arena to make the world a better place inspired, in part, Martin Luther King Jr., and is a point of inspiration to myself as well.

My experience with those pension boards set me on a course to advocate for diverse fund management and became a calling to take up Martin Luther King Jr.'s cause of economic justice. The more I worked on the issue, the more I realized what needed to be done. The work has become a personal mission, and I'm still fighting for it today.

Martin Luther King Jr.'s life is the ultimate example of stepping into the arena. In "Letter from Birmingham City Jail," he wrote to other clergy who claimed the Atlanta leader had no business organizing for civil rights in Birmingham, Alabama. King answered poignantly, writing, "I cannot sit idly by in Atlanta and not be concerned about what happens in Birmingham. Injustice anywhere is a threat to justice everywhere." In Birmingham and throughout his life, King made a conscious choice—to fight for racial justice no matter the terrain. He faced criticism from fellow clergy and "white moderates," whom he addressed in the Birmingham letter. He faced physical trials: pelted with rocks, stabbed, and jailed. Yet, none of that deterred him. "However difficult the moment, however frustrating the hour, it will not be long, because truth crushed to earth will rise again," he once said. I often reflect on his example in tough moments, reminding myself to keep pressing forward.

After entering the arena, I discovered I wasn't fighting alone. Others were committed to the fight for racial justice. Rich Dennis, founder of Sundial Brands, was one of the first in finance I met with a shared dedication to justice. One important initiative he's spearheaded is the New Voices initiative, which provides female entrepreneurs of color with the resources and capital they need to grow and succeed, empowering a new generation of business leaders. MacKenzie Scott, philanthropist and ex-wife of Jeff Bezos, is known for her generous donations and contributions to HBCUs, which train the bulk of Black professionals. These institutions have been strengthened so they can continue to train the next generation of African American professionals in business, law, medicine, and STEM. Corporate leaders like Rosalind Brewer, CEO of Walgreens Boots Alliance; Mellody Hobson, co-CEO of Ariel Investments; Tim Cook, CEO of Apple; Thasunda Brown Duckett, CEO of TIAA; and Meg Whitman, former CEO of Hewlett-Packard, championed diversity and inclusion in their companies, ensuring the next generation of leaders reflects the communities they serve. Bryan Stevenson, founder of the Equal Justice Initiative; Kimberlé Crenshaw, law professor and scholar in civil rights; Sharif El-Mekki, educator and advocate for school reform; and many more are making extraordinary strides in civil rights, education reform, and racial equity. Together, they're helping to build the more benevolent society King envisioned.

Fighting to build a more just world is deeply fulfilling, but it comes with its share of criticism. Critics are part of stepping into the arena. Dr. King faced slander, threats, and demagoguery. Yet, he understood something fundamental: Not all criticism carries the same weight. In his "Letter from Birmingham City Jail," he answered criticism from supporters with a caveat. "Seldom, if ever, do I pause to answer criticism of my work and ideas," he wrote. "But since I feel that you are men of genuine good will and your criticisms are sincerely set forth, I would like to answer your statement in what I hope will be patient and reasonable terms." He knew that some criticism stems from genuine concern, while others are distractions meant to slow progress. Being in the arena means learning to tell the difference between thoughtful critique and empty noise. If you're not in the fight for justice, your words carry little weight. But if you are in the arena with me, it's important to stay open to feedback from those who share your struggle.

Dr. King often sought counsel from his close friend and confidant, the late Harry Belafonte, a towering figure in the civil rights movement. In Belafonte's final years, I was privileged to form a meaningful friendship with him. In late 2019, Belafonte invited me to his apartment in New York. We sat down near a breathtaking Charles White painting of Mahalia Jackson. As I admired the masterpiece, Mr. Belafonte, in his melodic, raspy voice, began to share a story.

He recounted how before Dr. King took the stage at the March on Washington, Mahalia Jackson urged him to speak from his heart. "Tell them about the dream!" Jackson's encouragement led to the birth of the iconic "I Have a Dream" speech.

As our conversation shifted, Mr. Belafonte's demeanor grew serious. With a focused gaze, he spoke about the unfinished work of Dr. King—economic justice—and told me he wanted me to help carry that torch forward. It was one of the greatest honors of my life to have him entrust me with such an important mission.

Before I left, he motioned toward the painting of Mahalia and told me he wanted me to have it, to be the next steward of this masterwork as if to commemorate the legacy he was passing on to me. Today, that painting hangs in my ranch in Colorado, serving as a daily reminder of Harry Belafonte's generosity, his trust, and the enduring fight for justice.

Reflecting on my journey to the arena, I think we all face moments when our lives fork into two paths. One where we remain on the sidelines. One where we are called to fight for something that matters. I urge you that when that moment arises for you, to push past your fears and get into the arena. Ignore the critics and encourage others to do the same. When you enter this struggle, always remember that you are not alone. Others are fighting with you.

Dr. King believed that even small acts of courage could spark meaningful change. How can you make a lasting impact on the issues that matter most to you and your community?

Dr. King speaks at UC Berkeley's Sproul Plaza in Berkeley, California, May 17, 1967.

Michael Ochs Archives / Getty Images

7

A Call to Action

"I See the Promised Land"

Thank you very kindly, my friends. As I listened to Ralph Abernathy in his eloquent and generous introduction and then thought about myself, I wondered who he was talking about. It's always good to have your closest friend and associate say something good about you. And Ralph is the best friend that I have in the world.

I'm delighted to see each of you here tonight in spite of a storm warning. You reveal that you are determined to go on anyhow. Something is happening in Memphis; something is happening in our world.

As you know, if I were standing at the beginning of time, with the possibility of a general and panoramic view of the whole of human history up to now, and the Almighty said to me, "Martin Luther King, which age would you like to live in?"—I would take my mental flight by Egypt through, or rather across, the Red Sea, through the wilderness on toward the promised land. And in spite of its magnificence, I wouldn't stop there. I would move on by Greece and take my mind to Mount Olympus. And I would see Plato, Aristotle, Socrates, Euripides, and Aristophanes assembled around the Parthenon as they discussed the great and eternal issues of reality.

But I wouldn't stop there. I would go on, even to the great heyday of the Roman Empire. And I would see developments around there, through various emperors and leaders. But I wouldn't stop there. I would even come up to the day of the Renaissance, and get a quick picture of all that the Renaissance did for the cultural and aesthetic life of man. But I wouldn't stop there. I would even go by the way that the man for whom I'm named had his habitat. And I would watch Martin Luther as he tacked his Ninety-Five Theses on the door at the church in Wittenberg.

But I wouldn't stop there. I would come on up even to 1863, and watch a vacillating president by the name of Abraham Lincoln finally come to the conclusion that he had to sign the Emancipation Proclamation. But I wouldn't stop there. I would even come up to the early thirties, and see a man grappling with the problems of the bankruptcy of his nation. And come with an eloquent cry that we have nothing to fear but fear itself.

But I wouldn't stop there. Strangely enough, I would turn to the Almighty, and say, "If you allow me to live just a few years in the second half of the twentieth century, I will be happy." Now that's a strange statement to make, because the world is all messed up. The nation is sick. Trouble is in the land. Confusion all around. That's a strange statement. But I know, somehow, that only when it is dark enough can you see the stars. And I see God working in this period of the twentieth century in a way that men, in some strange way, are responding—something is happening in our world. The masses of people are rising up. And wherever they are assembled today, whether they are in Johannesburg, South Africa; Nairobi, Kenya; Accra, Ghana; New York City; Atlanta, Georgia; Jackson, Mississippi; or Memphis, Tennessee—the cry is always the same—"We want to be free."

And another reason that I'm happy to live in this period is that we have been forced to a point where we're going to have to grapple with the problems that men have been trying to grapple with through history, but the demands didn't force them to do it. Survival demands that we grapple with them. Men, for years now, have been talking about war and peace. But now, no longer can they just talk about it. It is no longer a choice between violence and nonviolence in this world; it's nonviolence or nonexistence.

That is where we are today. And also in the human rights revolution, if something isn't done, and in a hurry, to bring the colored peoples of the world out of their long years of poverty, their long years of hurt and neglect, the whole world is doomed. Now, I'm just happy that God has allowed me to live in this period, to see what is unfolding. And I'm happy that he's allowed me to be in Memphis.

I can remember, I can remember when Negroes were just going around as Ralph has said, so often, scratching where they didn't itch, and laughing when they were not tickled. But that day is all over. We mean business now, and we are determined to gain our rightful place in God's world.

And that's all this whole thing is about. We aren't engaged in any negative protest and in any negative arguments with anybody. We are saying that we are determined to be men. We are determined to be people. We are saying that we are God's children. And that we don't have to live like we are forced to live.

Now, what does all of this mean in this great period of history? It means that we've got to stay together. We've got to stay together and maintain unity. You know, whenever Pharaoh wanted to prolong the period of slavery in Egypt, he had a favorite, favorite formula for doing it. What was that? He kept the slaves fighting among themselves. But whenever the slaves get together, something happens in Pharaoh's court, and he cannot hold the slaves in slavery. When the slaves get together, that's the beginning of getting out of slavery. Now let us maintain unity.

Secondly, let us keep the issues where they are. The issue is injustice. The issue is the refusal of Memphis to be fair and honest in its dealings with its public servants, who happen to be sanitation workers. Now, we've got to keep attention on that. That's always the problem with a little violence. You know what happened the other day, and the press dealt only with the window-breaking. I read the articles. They very seldom got around to mentioning the fact that one thousand, three hundred sanitation workers were on strike, and that Memphis is not being fair to them, and that Mayor Loeb is in dire need of a doctor. They didn't get around to that.

Now we're going to march again, and we've got to march again, in order to put the issue where it is supposed to be. And force everybody to see that there are thirteen hundred of God's children here suffering, sometimes going hungry, going through dark and dreary nights wondering how this thing is going to come out. That's the issue. And we've got to say to the nation: "We know how it's coming out." For when people get caught up with that which is right and they are willing to sacrifice for it, there is no stopping point short of victory.

We aren't going to let any mace stop us. We are masters in our nonviolent movement in disarming police forces; they don't know what to do. I've seen them so often. I remember in Birmingham, Alabama, when we were in that majestic struggle there, we would move out of the 16th Street Baptist Church day after day; by the hundreds we would move out. And Bull Connor would tell them to send the dogs forth, and they did come; but we just went before the dogs singing, "Ain't gonna let nobody turn me round." Bull Connor next would say, "Turn the fire hoses on." And as I said to you the other night, Bull Connor didn't know history. He knew a kind of physics that somehow didn't relate to the transphysics that we knew about. And that was the fact that there was a certain kind of fire that no water could put out. And we went before the fire hoses; we had known water. If we were Baptist or some other denomination, we had been immersed. If we were Methodist, and some others, we had been sprinkled, but we knew water.

That couldn't stop us. And we just went on before the dogs and we would look at them; and we'd go on before the water hoses and we would look at it, and we'd just go on singing, "Over my head I see freedom in the air." And then we would be thrown in the paddy wagons, and sometimes we were stacked in there like sardines in a can. And they would throw us in, and old Bull would say, "Take them off," and they did; and we would just go in the paddy wagon singing, "We shall overcome." And every now and then we'd get in jail, and we'd see the jailers looking through the windows being moved by our prayers, and being moved by our words and our songs. And there was a power there which Bull

Connor couldn't adjust to; and so we ended up transforming Bull into a steer, and we won our struggle in Birmingham.

Now we've got to go on in Memphis just like that. I call upon you to be with us Monday. Now about injunctions: We have an injunction and we're going into court tomorrow morning to fight this illegal, unconstitutional injunction. All we say to America is, "Be true to what you said on paper." If I lived in China or even Russia, or any totalitarian country, maybe I could understand the denial of certain basic First Amendment privileges, because they hadn't committed themselves to that over there. But somewhere I read of the freedom of assembly. Somewhere I read of the freedom of speech. Somewhere I read of the freedom of the press. Somewhere I read that the greatness of America is the right to protest for right. And so just as I say, we aren't going to let any injunction turn us around. We are going on.

We need all of you. And you know what's beautiful to me, is to see all of these ministers of the gospel. It's a marvelous picture. Who is it that is supposed to articulate the longings and aspirations of the people more than the preacher? Somehow the preacher must be an Amos and say, "Let justice roll down like waters and righteousness like a mighty stream." Somehow, the preacher must say with Jesus, "The spirit of the Lord is upon me, because he hath anointed me to deal with the problems of the poor."

And I want to commend the preachers, under the leadership of these noble men: James Lawson, one who has been in this struggle for many years; he's been to jail for struggling, but he's still going on, fighting for the rights of his people. Rev. Ralph Jackson, Billy Kyles; I could just go right on down the list, but time will not permit. But I want to thank them all. And I want you to thank them, because so often, preachers aren't concerned about anything but themselves. And I'm always happy to see a relevant ministry.

It's alright to talk about "long white robes over yonder," in all of its symbolism. But ultimately people want some suits and dresses and shoes to wear down here. It's alright to talk about "streets flowing with milk and honey," but God has commanded us to be concerned about the slums down here, and his children who can't eat three square meals a day. It's alright to talk about the New Jerusalem, but one day, God's preacher must talk about the New York, the new Atlanta, the new Philadelphia, the new Los Angeles, the new Memphis, Tennessee. This is what we have to do.

Now the other thing we'll have to do is this: Always anchor our external direct action with the power of economic withdrawal. Now, we are poor people, individually; we are poor when you compare us with white society in America. We are poor. Never stop and forget that collectively, that means all of us together, collectively we are richer than all the nations in the world, with the exception of nine. Did you ever think about that? After you leave the United States, Soviet Russia, Great

Britain, West Germany, France, and I could name the others, the Negro collectively is richer than most nations of the world. We have an annual income of more than thirty billion dollars a year, which is more than all of the exports of the United States, and more than the national budget of Canada. Did you know that? That's power right there, if we know how to pool it.

We don't have to argue with anybody. We don't have to curse and go around acting bad with our words. We don't need any bricks and bottles, we don't need any Molotov cocktails, we just need to go around to these stores, and to these massive industries in our country, and say, "God sent us by here to say to you that you're not treating his children right. And we've come by here to ask you to make the first item on your agenda fair treatment, where God's children are concerned. Now, if you are not prepared to do that, we do have an agenda that must follow. And our agenda calls for withdrawing economic support from you."

And so, as a result of this, we are asking you tonight, to go out and tell your neighbors not to buy Coca-Cola in Memphis. Go by and tell them not to buy Sealtest milk. Tell them not to buy—what is the other bread?—Wonder Bread. And what is the other bread company, Jesse? Tell them not to buy Hart's bread. As Jesse Jackson has said, up to now, only the garbage men have been feeling pain; now we must kind of redistribute the pain. We are choosing these companies because they haven't been fair in their hiring practices; and we are choosing them because they can begin the process of saying they are going to support the needs and the rights of these men who are on strike. And then they can move on downtown and tell Mayor Loeb to do what is right.

But not only that, we've got to strengthen Black institutions. I call upon you to take your money out of the banks downtown and deposit your money in Tri-State Bank—we want a "bank-in" movement in Memphis. So go by the savings and loan association. I'm not asking you something that we don't do ourselves at SCLC. Judge Hooks and others will tell you that we have an account here in the savings and loan association from the Southern Christian Leadership Conference. We're just telling you to follow what we're doing. Put your money there. You have six or seven Black insurance companies in Memphis. Take out your insurance there. We want to have an "insurance-in."

Now these are some practical things we can do. We begin the process of building a greater economic base. And at the same time, we are putting pressure where it really hurts. I ask you to follow through here.

Now, let me say as I move to my conclusion that we've got to give ourselves to this struggle until the end. Nothing would be more tragic than to stop at this point, in Memphis. We've got to see it through. And when we have our march, you need to be there. Be concerned about your brother. You may not be on strike. But either we go up together, or we go down together.

Let us develop a kind of dangerous unselfishness. One day a man came to Jesus; and he wanted to raise some questions about some vital matters in life. At points, he wanted to trick Jesus, and show him that he knew a little more than Jesus knew, and through this, throw him off base. Now that question could have easily ended up in a philosophical and theological debate. But Jesus immediately pulled that question from midair, and placed it on a dangerous curve between Jerusalem and Jericho. And he talked about a certain man who fell among thieves. You remember that a Levite and a priest passed by on the other side. They didn't stop to help him. And finally a man of another race came by. He got down from his beast, decided not to be compassionate by proxy. But with him, administered first aid, and helped the man in need. Jesus ended up saying this was the good man, this was the great man, because he had the capacity to project the "I" into the "thou," and to be concerned about his brother. Now you know, we use our imagination a great deal to try to determine why the priest and the Levite didn't stop. At times we say they were busy going to church meetings—an ecclesiastical gathering—and they had to get on down to Jerusalem so they wouldn't be late for their meeting. At other times we would speculate that there was a religious law that "one who was engaged in religious ceremonies was not to touch a human body twenty-four hours before the ceremony." And every now and then we begin to wonder whether maybe they were not going down to Jerusalem, or down to Jericho, rather to organize a "Jericho Road Improvement Association." That's a possibility. Maybe they felt that it was better to deal with the problem from the causal root, rather than to get bogged down with the individual effort.

But I'm going to tell you what my imagination tells me. It's possible that these men were afraid. You see, the Jericho road is a dangerous road. I remember when Mrs. King and I were first in Jerusalem. We rented a car and drove from Jerusalem down to Jericho. And as soon as we got on that road, I said to my wife, "I can see why Jesus used this as a setting for his parable." It's a winding, meandering road. It's really conducive for ambushing. You start out in Jerusalem, which is about 1,200 miles, or rather 1,200 feet above sea level. And by the time you get down to Jericho, fifteen or twenty minutes later, you're about 2,200 feet below sea level. That's a dangerous road. In the days of Jesus it came to be known as the "Bloody Pass." And you know, it's possible that the priest and the Levite looked over that man on the ground and wondered if the robbers were still around. Or it's possible that they felt that the man on the ground was merely faking. And he was acting like he had been robbed and hurt, in order to seize them over there, lure them there for quick and easy seizure. And so the first question that the Levite asked was, "If I stop to help this man, what will happen to me?" But then the Good Samaritan came by. And he reversed the question: "If I do not stop to help this man, what will happen to him?"

That's the question before you tonight. Not, "If I stop to help the sanitation workers, what will happen to all of the hours that I usually spend in my office every day and every week as a pastor?" The question is not, "If I stop to help this man in need, what will happen to me?" "If I do not stop to help the sanitation workers, what will happen to them?" That's the question.

Let us rise up tonight with a greater readiness. Let us stand with a greater determination. And let us move on in these powerful days, these days of challenge to make America what it ought to be. We have an opportunity to make America a better nation. And I want to thank God, once more, for allowing me to be here with you.

You know, several years ago, I was in New York City autographing the first book that I had written. And while sitting there autographing books, a demented Black woman came up. The only question I heard from her was, "Are you Martin Luther King?"

And I was looking down writing, and I said yes. And the next minute I felt something beating on my chest. Before I knew it I had been stabbed by this demented woman. I was rushed to Harlem Hospital. It was a dark Saturday afternoon. And that blade had gone through, and the X-rays revealed that the tip of the blade was on the edge of my aorta, the main artery. And once that's punctured, you drown in your own blood—that's the end of you.

It came out in *The New York Times* the next morning, that if I had sneezed, I would have died. Well, about four days later, they allowed me, after the operation, after my chest had been opened, and the blade had been taken out, to move around in the wheelchair in the hospital. They allowed me to read some of the mail that came in, and from all over the states, and the world, kind letters came in. I read a few, but one of them I will never forget. I had received one from the president and the vice president. I've forgotten what those telegrams said. I'd received a visit and a letter from the governor of New York, but I've forgotten what the letter said. But there was another letter that came from a little girl, a young girl who was a student at the White Plains High School. And I looked at that letter, and I'll never forget it. It said simply, "Dear Dr. King: I am a ninth-grade student at the White Plains High School." She said, "While it should not matter, I would like to mention that I am a white girl. I read in the paper of your misfortune, and of your suffering. And I read that if you had sneezed, you would have died. And I'm simply writing you to say that I'm so happy that you didn't sneeze."

And I want to say tonight, I want to say that I am happy that I didn't sneeze. Because if I had sneezed, I wouldn't have been around here in 1960, when students all over the South started sitting-in at lunch counters. And I knew that as they were sitting in, they were really standing up for the best in the American dream. And taking the whole nation back to those great wells of democracy which were dug deep by the Founding Fathers in the Declaration of Independence and the Constitution. If I had sneezed, I wouldn't have been around in 1962, when Negroes in Albany, Georgia, decided to straighten their backs up. And whenever men and women straighten their backs up, they are going somewhere, because a man can't ride your back unless it is bent. If I had sneezed, I wouldn't have been here in 1963, when the Black people of Birmingham, Alabama, aroused the conscience of this nation, and brought into being the civil rights bill. If I had sneezed, I wouldn't have had a chance later that year, in August, to try to tell Americans about a dream that I had had. If I had sneezed, I wouldn't have been down in Selma, Alabama, to see the great movement there. If I had sneezed, I wouldn't have been in Memphis to see a community rally around those brothers and sisters who are suffering. I'm so happy that I didn't sneeze.

And they were telling me, now it doesn't matter now. It really doesn't matter what happens now. I left Atlanta this morning, and as we got started on the plane, there were six of us, the pilot said over the public address system, "We are sorry for the delay, but we have Dr. Martin Luther King on the plane. And to be sure that all of the bags were checked, and to be sure that nothing would be wrong with the plane, we had to check out everything carefully. And we've had the plane protected and guarded all night."

And then I got into Memphis. And some began to say the threats, or talk about the threats that were out. What would happen to me from some of our sick white brothers?

Well, I don't know what will happen now. We've got some difficult days ahead. But it doesn't matter with me now. Because I've been to the mountaintop. And I don't mind. Like anybody, I would like to live a long life. Longevity has its place. But I'm not concerned about that now. I just want to do God's will. And he's allowed me to go up to the mountain. And I've looked over. And I've seen the promised land. I may not get there with you. But I want you to know tonight that we, as a people, will get to the promised land. And I'm happy, tonight. I'm not worried about anything. I'm not fearing any man. "Mine eyes have seen the glory of the coming of the Lord."

—Martin Luther King, Jr.

April 3, 1968, Memphis, Tennessee

> Dr. King was taken from us shortly after delivering his powerful "I See the Promised Land" speech. In that speech, he urged people to keep fighting for justice, even if he was no longer here to lead us. In the spirit of fighting on in Dr. King's memory, I want to offer steps we can all take to advance economic justice.

It was his final speech. On a hot summer evening inside a packed church auditorium in Memphis, Dr. King fatefully presaged, "I may not get there with you, but I want you to know tonight that we, as a people, will get to the promised land." In his last years, before his life was cut short, Dr. King aspired to build on his work to outlaw segregation and codify voting rights. He dreamed of creating a fairer education system and an economy where everyone could succeed.

As the inheritors of his legacy and vision, it's now up to us to complete the work of fighting for greater economic justice. If we work together, we can build a new type of Beloved Community, one focused on creating a more benevolent, more equitable society. Here are some of the most impactful things you can do to join in furthering Dr. King's economic justice legacy.

Help Close the Racial Wealth Gap

In his 1968 Memphis speech, Dr. King spoke about the need for Black people to focus on economic justice. He said, "We begin the process of building a greater economic base. And at the same time, we are putting pressure where it hurts. I ask you to follow through here." Nearly six decades later, the rate of Black unemployment is twice as high as it is for white Americans, Black business formation and homeownership still lags, and the racial wealth gap persists, with Black households having around one-twelfth of the wealth of whites. We need to take steps to close the gaps in financial knowledge and access to capital to have the greatest impact.

The good news is that there are specific steps we can take to reduce this gap. First, we need to prioritize educating ourselves and those around us on personal finance, economics, and wealth creation. You can start by taking personal finance classes at your local community center, church, or online, or by reading books like *Standing at the Scratch Line* by Guy Johnson, *The Wealth Choice* by Dennis Kimbro, and *Principles* by Ray Dalio, or listening to podcasts like *Earn Your Leisure* and *Planet Money*.

Consider starting a book club or investment group. My interest in finance began as a young engineer in a book club with my peers. If you're already financially literate, share that knowledge. Mentor others. Teach financial literacy in your community or volunteer at local schools. Raising the financial knowledge base of our communities is essential, but it's only the first step.

One of the most significant ways to close the racial wealth gap is by increasing access to capital for underbanked, underinvested, and undercapitalized communities. Capital is the economic lifeblood needed to spur business formation, charitable work, homeownership, and investment. Seventy percent of communities of color don't have a bank branch of any kind, so the best tool we have right now to increase capital access is Community Development Financial Institutions. There are more than 1,500 CDFIs in America. These organizations provide vital services like business loans, mortgage loans, and banking services, which are crucial in underbanked communities like northeast Denver, where I grew up.

If you care about bolstering CDFIs, you can rally institutions you're a part of to support them. For example, advocating for the companies, universities, or nonprofits you're a part of to invest in CDFIs can build their capital base by providing primary equity. Or you could encourage your organization to help modernize CDFI operations by upgrading their technology. If you're in a position of influence, you could make it a priority for your organization to support CDFIs. I established the Southern Communities Initiative in partnership with the CEO of the Kellogg Foundation, Boston Consulting Group, and PayPal to support this work. If you would like more information on this vital issue, you can visit our website at SouthernCommunitiesInitiative.com.

Another important action you can take is to support Black-owned businesses. Black consumers spend $910 billion annually, making the businesses that serve Black people and communities vital to economic growth and empowerment. Black-owned enterprises are centers of job creation, innovation, and cultural preservation, and they strengthen the broader economy. If you're in a leadership position, seek out Black-owned vendors. Work with them and consider mentoring them to help them grow and expand alongside you. Also, engage with the charitable arms of the organizations where you work and have influence, and encourage them to donate to and support nonprofits that uplift Black-owned businesses or entrepreneurs. Advocate for your company to enroll in a matching gifts program and match employee contributions to organizations that support Black-owned businesses. On a personal level, you can make intentional choices as a consumer and investor. Whether it's holiday shopping or selecting a financial planner, every dollar spent with Black-owned businesses creates a ripple effect of opportunity. By directing that spending toward Black-owned businesses, we can create sustainable change.

Fight for Broadband Equity

I keep coming back to the fact that Black Americans have been excluded from every major economic boom, and the ramifications of those exclusions have been generational. That's why we must include Black Americans in the tech boom. In order to do so, Black communities need access to broadband and STEM education. General-purpose technology access unlocks productivity. Generative AI has proven to be one of the most powerful catalysts for the digital economy, and mastering this capability will be essential for ensuring sustainable economic power. Similarly, broadband access enables key productivity tools like online education, banking, commerce, and telehealth, all of which are critical to advancing economic opportunity.

Our government spends significant amounts of money on national broadband infrastructure and services. This is a vital funding stream for the improvements our communities require. Contact your elected officials and push for broadband funds, like those from the Broadband Equity, Access & Deployment (BEAD) Program, to be directed to communities of color where high-speed internet is urgently needed. Leave a message with your senators' and congressperson's offices, contact the White House, attend town halls and speak up, or even organize a civic action. There will be a significant investment in broadband access in the coming years, and we must raise our voices together to ensure it's done equitably and that Black communities are included. Student Freedom Initiative is advancing this work. If you'd like more information, go to studentfreedominitiative.org.

EQUIP AFRICAN AMERICANS WITH STEM TRAINING

Broadband access is just the beginning. To succeed in the tech-driven economy, Black workers need skills in STEM fields. If you're tech-savvy, find an organization where you can share your knowledge, such as NPower. If you're not, now is the time to learn. Take online courses, attend workshops, or join a coding boot camp. Support organizations like Girls Who Code, Black Girls Code, or Code.org, which are preparing the next generation of Black tech leaders.

Historically Black Colleges and Universities (HBCUs) are among the most important institutions for upskilling Black people in STEM. As discussed earlier, these institutions have historically trained the bulk of Black professionals and will continue to lead the way in STEM. Institutions like Morehouse, Spelman, and North Carolina A&T are training the next wave of Black innovators in AI, cyber-security, and data science. If you're in business or tech, don't overlook HBCUs when recruiting new hires. It could be rewarding to partner with them to strengthen their curriculum and create opportunities for their students.

Building on my Morehouse gift in 2019, I founded the Student Freedom Initiative (SFI) to help African American students overcome financial barriers to education, particularly in the tech sector. SFI provides income-contingent, forgivable, low-interest college loans. Additionally, SFI is investing in HBCU infrastructure, making enhancements to cybersecurity programs, and upgrading campus facilities. They are also creating internship opportunities in cutting-edge fields like solar energy.

I will never forget how my mother wrote a check to the United Negro College Fund (UNCF) in our kitchen every month. She was determined to support African Americans pursuing an education. You can make a difference by donating to UNCF or other Black education nonprofits and scholarships.

As a young man, I landed an internship at Bell Labs, which set me on my path in STEM and opened doors for me. I know firsthand the power of an internship, so I founded internXL, a program that finds and trains talented young people of color to fill internships. Today, internXL is expanding its reach to include other underserved groups, such as Indigenous populations in the US and Canada, as well as Southeast Asians and individuals from the Middle East. The program has connected over twenty-three thousand students with internships at over three hundred companies. If you're interested in recruiting more diverse talent for your company, reach out to internXL. We will help you find talent.

Advocate for Diversity in Pension Fund Management

Pension funds represent one of the largest pools of capital in the world, with a global value of $126 trillion. In the US alone, pension funds account for trillions in worker savings. Despite minorities making up a significant portion of the workforce and pensioners, the majority of their savings are managed by people who don't look like them. According to the National Association of Investment Companies (NAIC), people of color comprise nearly a third of the workforce, yet people of color control only around 14 percent of investment assets and just 9 percent of public pension funds. Even more concerning, it's estimated that women- and minority-owned firms oversee just 1.4 percent of the total assets under management in the US—despite women and people of color making up 70 percent of the US working-age population.

This is particularly distressing because managers of color consistently outperform their peers. NAIC research shows that firms led by managers of color deliver strong returns, often beating traditional benchmarks. McKinsey & Company's 2020 report found that companies in the top quartile for ethnic and cultural diversity are 36 percent more likely to have above-average profitability, and diverse teams drive more innovation. Additionally, managers of color are more likely to invest in minority-owned businesses and companies operating in Black and Latinx communities, contributing directly to economic growth in those areas.

I wonder what Dr. King would think about the fact that the savings of Black workers, like the sanitation workers he stood with in Memphis, are often funneled into companies that harm their communities, such as private prison companies and predatory lending institutions. This is why diversity in pension fund management is so critical.

What can you do to help change this? If you're a public employee or a union member, join your union or company's pension boards or investment committees. Advocate for investment strategies that prioritize a diversity of fund managers and promote inclusive investment approaches based on performance. Genuine economic justice means the percentage of pension funds invested in managers of color should reflect diversity of workers contributing to those funds.

BUILD COMMUNITY

In northeast Denver, where I grew up, we didn't just organize for better education or to get the streets cleared. We came together for backyard fish fries, fishing trips and nature excursions in Lincoln Hills, and Memorial Day parades to honor our vets and Tuskegee Airmen in our community. Dr. King reminded us that joy and cultural preservation were critical, even amid the struggle.

I encourage you to support organizations that foster community and cultural preservation, like Lincoln Hills Cares or Foster Love. Cultural institutions like Carnegie Hall, Sphinx Organization, and the Louis Armstrong House Museum celebrate Black artistry. Volunteer, donate, or show up to support their work. And don't forget the importance of nature in community building—whether it's parks, outdoor spaces, or conservation efforts. Connecting with nature is crucial, especially for youth and African Americans who live in urban environments. Supporting organizations like the National Park Service, the Black Outdoors, or the African American Nature and Heritage Tour helps ensure that everyone has access to our shared natural heritage. These groups work to preserve and promote spaces that are significant to Black history and culture, ensuring that these natural treasures remain accessible for future generations.

ADVOCATE FOR RACIAL JUSTICE

Dr. King's fight didn't end with civil rights. He demanded justice in legal and political systems. If you feel called to this work, get involved with organizations like RE-Alliance or Justice for Black Girls, which are fighting for equity in our legal systems. Whether through donations, volunteering, or raising awareness, your support brings us closer to realizing Dr. King's vision of equality.

Today, we are witnessing attacks on affirmative action and DEI initiatives. The facts are clear: Diverse workforces drive innovation and create more substantial organizations. For example, companies with diverse management teams are 33 percent more likely to see higher profits. Moreover, businesses with inclusive cultures are 1.7 times more likely to be innovation leaders in their market. Even if you're not in a leadership role, advocate for DEI in your workplace. Join resource groups, mentor others, and push for inclusive policies because they lead to better business outcomes. According to the overwhelming amount of data, prioritizing diversity is not just a moral imperative but a fiduciary responsibility. Failure to do so risks neglecting this critical aspect of business success.

Dr. King famously said, "The arc of the moral universe is long, but it bends toward justice." That trajectory doesn't bend by itself; it changes because we actively push and pull it in the right direction. Getting involved in boards and committees that control capital decisions is one of the most impactful ways to contribute. Whether it's a pension board, an investment committee, a decision-maker who can hire diverse vendors and create internships that recruit from HBCUs, or a corporate board, these positions hold the keys to where resources are allocated. By stepping into these roles, you can help direct funds to where they are most needed, ensuring they uplift all communities, not just a select few. Let's roll up our sleeves and take this step together. I would be honored if you would join me in the fight to fulfill Dr. King's dream of economic justice for all.

These are some key ways we can advance Dr. King's vision for economic justice, though this is by no means an exhaustive list. The most important thing is that you carry forward his mission in your own way.

What actions will you take to make
a meaningful difference in your
community? Reflecting on the causes
you care about, what specific steps
can you take to advance these efforts
and ensure broader participation
in economic opportunities? How
will you hold yourself accountable
for making progress? Embrace
that power and take action.

Engage allies, build bridges, and create meaningful connections. It's up to you to harness that power and make the changes that will impact your life and the condition of your community. What will your next steps be, and how will you measure your progress in creating lasting change?

Epilogue

We are enough to . . .

Make our communities safe

Make our votes count

Make our water safe to drink and our food nutritious

Make our politicians represent our interests

Educate our children so they can be productive,

enlightened citizens of Humanity

Stabilize our neighborhoods

Provide fresh clean air and access to God's great outdoors

Empower our sons and daughters to be enough to fulfill their dreams

Teach our children ways of living that make God's glorious planet

live and thrive rather than wither and withstand.

–Robert F. Smith

Acknowledgments

This book—and my life—were made possible by my family and innumerable visionaries who sacrificed greatly for a more perfect union. At the top of this list are my parents, Dr. Sylvia Myrna Smith and Dr. William Robert Smith; their loving siblings, including my aunt Linda, who form the center of our Beloved Community in Denver; and many other family and community members who fortified my self-worth, indulged my curiosity, and nurtured my aspirations. My wife, Hope, and my children, Zoe, Eliana, Max, Legend, Hendrix, Zuri, and Zya, rekindle my dreams each day and carry forward the important work of caring for each other and for the world at large.

Others to whom I'll forever be indebted include Dr. King; his contemporaries, including Reverend Sharpton, John Lewis, Elijah Cummings, and Jim Clyburn; and the countless mentors they inspired, including Ray Maguire, John Utendahl, Bernard Tyson, and Dick Parsons. I'd also like to express my gratitude to the educators, medical and safety and sanitation personnel, farm and factory workers, community and social service organizers, artists, and millions of others worldwide whose often invisible labor enables each of our lives.

In addition: Ibram Kendi and Shomari Wills were enormously helpful with the writing process; my chief of staff, Ami Desai, developed and executed this entire project; and HarperCollins and the King Estate continue to share Dr. King's ideas with future generations. Thank you to my colleagues at Vista Equity Partners, who embody excellence and service; Maria Nicolas, my longtime executive assistant; and the talented teams at Fund II Foundation, Student Freedom Initiative, internXL, Southern Communities Initiative, Prostate Cancer Foundation, Mt. Sinai, Carnegie Hall, Sphinx, National Park Foundation, Conference of National Black Churches, National Action Network, Urban League, NAACP and the Legal Defense Fund, Black Economic Alliance, National Association of Investment Companies, National Bankers Association, Girls Who Code, Girls Who Invest, Toigo Foundation, and Alvin Ailey Dance Company, who embody the ideals of Dr. King and America itself.

Notes

CHAPTER 1: LET FREEDOM RING FROM THE SNOW-CAPPED ROCKIES

9   "We've come to our nation's capital to cash a check": Martin Luther King Jr., "I Have a Dream," speech delivered at the March on Washington for Jobs and Freedom, August 28, 1963, Lincoln Memorial, Washington, DC.

10 "the other America": Martin Luther King Jr., "The Other America," speech delivered at Stanford University, April 14, 1967, Stanford, CA.

12 "I have a dream": King, "I Have a Dream."

12 "Five score years ago": King, "I Have a Dream."

12 "robbed, by his master": Frederick Douglass, *My Bondage and My Freedom* (Miller, Orton & Mulligan, 1855), 219.

13 "the black man's cow": Frederick Douglass, *The Life and Times of Frederick Douglass* (De Wolfe & Fiske Co., 1892), 275.

14 A 2022 study by Brandeis University: Tatjana Meschede et al., "Final Report from IERE's GI Bill Study," Institute for

Economic and Racial Equity, Brandeis University, December 2022, https://heller.brandeis.edu/iere/pdfs/racial-wealth-equity/racial-wealth-gap/gi-bill-final-report.pdf.

15   "We've come to our nation's capital to cash a check": King, "I Have a Dream."

15   "insufficient funds": King, "I Have a Dream."

15   "the Negro lives on a lonely island of poverty": King, "I Have a Dream."

15   "We refuse to believe that there are insufficient funds": King, "I Have a Dream."

16   "Let freedom ring": King, "I Have a Dream."

16   "As we walk, we must make the pledge": King, "I Have a Dream."

Chapter 2: The Beloved Community

37   "Our objective is to cultivate a Beloved Community": Martin Luther King Jr., "Justice Without Violence," Brandeis University, Waltham, MA, April 3, 1957.

39   "unique in its magnitude": Sadie Gurman, "Justice Department Report Aims to Correct Record on Tulsa Race Massacre," *Wall Street Journal*, January 11, 2025, https://www.wsj.com/us-news/law/justice-department-report-aims-to-correct-record-on-tulsa-race-massacre-3e8fcfb1.

41 During World Wars I and II: "African American Troops Fought to Fight in World War I," US Department of Defense, accessed May 6, 2025, https://www.defense.gov/News/News-Stories /Article/article/1429624/african-american-troops-fought-to -fight-in-world-war-i/; "Honoring Black History World War II Service to the Nation," US Army, accessed May 6, 2025, https:// www.army.mil/article/233117/honoring_black_history_world _war_ii_service_to_the_nation; "Buffalo Soldiers in the Korean War," National Park Service, accessed May 6, 2025, https://www.nps.gov/chyo/learn/historyculture/busokoreanwar .htm; "Vietnam War US Military Fatal Casualty Statistics," National Archives, accessed May 6, 2025, https://www.archives .gov/research/military/vietnam-war/casualty-statistics.

43 more than 99 percent of their students: SEO USA, "Our Programs," SEO, accessed November 18, 2024, https://www .seo-usa.org/our-programs/.

44 At the time, Black Americans: US Census Bureau, *1970 Census of Population and Housing*, US Government Printing Office, 1972, and 2020 Census Data, US Government Printing Office, 2021.

46 "Each of us must do our part": John Lewis, *Across That Bridge: Life Lessons and a Vision for Change* (Hyperion, 2012), 122.

46 "When you see something that is not right": Lewis, *Across That Bridge*, 75.

CHAPTER 3: THE TWO AMERICAS

75   African American college graduates today: "On Views of Race
     and Inequality, Blacks and Whites Are Worlds Apart," Pew
     Research Center, June 27, 2016, https://www.pewresearch.org
     /social-trends/2016/06/27/on-views-of-race-and-inequality
     -blacks-and-whites-are-worlds-apart/.

76   The kids in my community who weren't bused: Rucker C.
     Johnson, "Long-Run Impacts of School Desegregation & School
     Quality on Adult Attainments," NBER Working Paper No.
     16664, National Bureau of Economic Research, January 2011;
     revised September 2015, https://www.nber.org/papers/w16664.

76   School districts serving predominantly Black communities: Ary
     Spatig-Amerikaner, "Unequal Education: Federal Loophole
     Enables Lower Spending on Students of Color," Center for
     American Progress, 2012, 4, https://uncf.org/wp-content/uploads
     /PDFs/UnequalEduation.pdf.

76   After high school, African American kids: National Center
     for Education Statistics, "College Participation Rates for 18- to
     24-Year-Olds," US Department of Education, 2024, https://
     nces.ed.gov/programs/coe/pdf/coe_cpb.pdf.

76   Only 27 percent of Black Americans hold college degrees: "Key
     Facts About Black Americans," Pew Research Center, January
     23, 2025, https://www.pewresearch.org/short-reads/2025/01/23
     /key-facts-about-black-americans/.

77 the University of Amherst and MIT: American Bar Association, "ABA Required Disclosures: 2024 Law School Admissions Data," accessed May 6, 2025, https://www.abarequireddisclosures.org.

77 Harvard Law School admitted: American Bar Association, "ABA Required Disclosures."

77 African American college students borrow nearly double: Ben Miller, "The Continued Student Loan Crisis for Black Borrowers," Center for American Progress, December 2, 2019, https://www.americanprogress.org/article/continued-student -loan-crisis-black-borrowers/.

78 African Americans having a net worth ten times less than whites: Rakesh Kochhar and Mohamad Moslimani, "Wealth Surged in the Pandemic, but Debt Endures for Poorer Black and Hispanic Families," Pew Research Center, December 4, 2023, https:// www.pewresearch.org/race-and-ethnicity/2023/12/04 /wealth-surged-in-the-pandemic-but-debt-endures-for-poorer -black-and-hispanic-families/.

CHAPTER 4: ECONOMIC JUSTICE

101 lower wages and higher unemployment: Olugbenga Ajilore, "On the Persistence of the Black-White Unemployment Gap," Center for American Progress, February 24, 2020, https://www .americanprogress.org/article/persistence-black-white -unemployment-gap/.

102   45 percent of Black families: Alexander Hermann, "In Nearly
      Every State, People of Color Are Less Likely to Own Homes
      Compared to White Households," Joint Center for Housing
      Studies of Harvard University, February 8, 2023, https://www
      .jchs.harvard.edu/blog/nearly-every-state-people-color-are-less
      -likely-own-homes-compared-white-households.

103   they often have lower values: Hermann, "In Nearly Every State."

103   student loan payments consume: Andre M. Perry, Marshall
      Steinbaum, and Carl Romer, "Student Loans, the Racial Wealth
      Divide, and Why We Need Full Student Debt Cancellation,"
      Brookings Institution, June 23, 2021, https://www.brookings
      .edu/articles/student-loans-the-racial-wealth-divide-and-why
      -we-need-full-student-debt-cancellation/.

103   résumés with "Black-sounding" names: Marianne Bertrand and
      Sendhil Mullainathan, "Are Emily and Greg More Employable
      than Lakisha and Jamal? A Field Experiment on Labor Market
      Discrimination," National Bureau of Economic Research, July
      2003, https://doi.org/10.3386/w9873.

104   white workers earn almost 25 percent more: Mary C. Daly,
      Bart Hobijn, and Joseph H. Pedtke, "Disappointing Facts
      about the Black-White Wage Gap," FRBSF Economic Letter,
      September 5, 2017, https://www.frbsf.org/research-and-insights
      /publications/economic-letter/2017/09/disappointing-facts
      -about-black-white-wage-gap/.

104 Black Americans are more likely to be union members: US
     Bureau of Labor Statistics, "Union Members Summary—2024
     A01 Results," January 28, 2025, https://www.bls.gov/news
     .release/union2.nr0.htm.

104 Only around 2 percent of fund managers are Black: Knight
     Foundation, "Diversity of Asset Managers Research Series: Asset
     Management Industry," March 4, 2021, https://knightfoundation
     .org/reports/knight-diversity-of-asset-managers-research-series
     -industry/.

105 When Black Americans apply for loans: Federal Reserve Banks,
     "2022 Report on Firms Owned by People of Color: Based on
     the 2021 Small Business Credit Survey," June 29, 2022, https://
     doi.org/10.55350/sbcs-20220629.

105 more than one in four African Americans are underbanked:
     Federal Reserve Board, "Economic Well-Being of US
     Households in 2020: Banking and Credit," May 2021, https://
     www.federalreserve.gov/publications/2021-economic-well
     -being-of-us-households-in-2020-executive-summary.htm.

107 Black Americans were less likely than white Americans to be
     beneficiaries: Sarah Turner and John Bound, "The GI Bill,
     World War II, and the Education of Black Americans," National
     Bureau of Economic Research Digest, December 2002, https://
     www.nber.org/digest/dec02/gi-bill-world-war-ii-and-education
     -black-americans.

107 the federal government has earmarked $42.25 billion:
"Broadband Equity, Access, and Deployment (BEAD)
Program," BroadbandUSA, National Telecommunications
and Information Administration, accessed March 28, 2025,
https://broadbandusa.ntia.doc.gov/funding-programs
/broadband-equity-access-and-deployment-bead-program.

108 40 percent of African Americans currently without access:
Sara Atske and Andrew Perrin, "Home Broadband
Adoption, Computer Ownership Vary by Race, Ethnicity in
the US," Pew Research Center, July 16, 2021, https://www
.pewresearch.org/short-reads/2021/07/16/home-broadband
-adoption-computer-ownership-vary-by-race-ethnicity-in
-the-u-s/.

108 around 80 percent of HBCU students: Susan Aud, Mary Ann
Fox, and Angelina KewalRamani, "Status and Trends in the
Education of Racial and Ethnic Groups," National Center for
Education Statistics, July 2010, https://nces.ed.gov/pubs2010
/2010015.pdf.

110 "a new kind of Selma or Birmingham": Martin Luther King Jr.,
"Statement by Martin Luther King Jr. on the Poor People's
Campaign, December 4, 1967," Joseph Echols and Evelyn
Gibson Lowery Collection, Atlanta University Center Robert W.
Woodruff Library, http://hdl.handle.net/20.500.12322
/auc.199:08266.

CHAPTER 5: ALLIES

124 "There are Hitlers loose in America today": Martin Luther King
     Jr., "Address to the American Jewish Congress," Miami, Florida,
     May 14, 1958.

125 Rosenwald partnered with Booker T. Washington: Jesse
     Steinmetz, "The Enduring Legacy of Rosenwald Schools in
     Charlotte and Throughout the American South," WFAE 90.7,
     January 13, 2022, https://www.wfae.org/show/charlotte-talks
     -with-mike-collins/2022–01–12/the-enduring-legacy-of
     -rosenwald-schools-in-charlotte-and-throughout-the
     -american-south; Michael J. Solender, "How the Rosenwald
     Schools Shaped a Generation of Black Leaders," *Smithsonian
     Magazine*, March 30, 2021, https://www.smithsonianmag.com
     /history/how-rosenwald-schools-shaped-legacy-generation
     -black-leaders-180977340/.

125 these schools educated one-third of Black children: Steinmetz,
     "The Enduring Legacy;" Solender, "How the Rosenwald
     Schools."

125 according to the Prussian Memorandum: The Prussian
     Memorandum, as discussed in James Q. Whitman, *Hitler's
     American Model: The United States and the Making of Nazi Race Law*
     (Princeton University Press, 2017), 2, 31–35, 75–79.

127 "The most important thing I learned": Joachim Prinz, "The
     Problem of Silence," speech at the March on Washington,

August 28, 1963, https://www.americanjewisharchives.org
/snapshots/the-problem-of-silence-rabbi-joachim-prinz
-speech-at-the-march-on-washington/.

128 With the US having one of the highest incarceration rates:
Paola Scommegna, "US Has World's Highest Incarceration
Rate," Population Reference Bureau, August 10, 2012, https://
www.prb.org/resources/u-s-has-worlds-highest-incarceration
-rate/.

Chapter 6: Man in the Arena

163 only about 1.4 percent: John S. and James L. Knight Foundation,
"Asset Management Industry Severely Lacking Diversity, New
Knight Foundation Study Finds; Signals Untapped Opportunity
For Investors," The Knight Foundation, December 7, 2021,
https://knightfoundation.org/press/releases/asset-management
-industry-severely-lacking-diversity-new-knight-foundation
-study-finds-signals-untapped-opportunity-for-investors/.

164 "The credit belongs": Theodore Roosevelt, "Citizenship in a
Republic," speech, Sorbonne, Paris, April 23, 1910, https://
theodoreroosevelt.org/content.aspx?page_id=22&club
_id=991271&module_id=339364.

164 "However difficult the moment": Martin Luther King Jr., "The
Montgomery Bus Boycott," delivered December 5, 1955.

CHAPTER 7: A CALL TO ACTION

187   "I may not get there with you": Martin Luther King Jr., "I See
      the Promised Land," speech delivered at Mason Temple, April 3,
      1968, Memphis, TN.

188   "We begin the process of building a greater economic base": King,
      "I See the Promised Land."

188   The rate of Black unemployment is twice as high: Olugbenga
      Ajilore, "On the Persistence of the Black-White Unemployment
      Gap," Center for American Progress, February 24, 2020, https://
      www.americanprogress.org/article/persistence
      -black-white-unemployment-gap/.

188   Black households having around one-twelfth: Rakesh Kochhar
      and Mohamad Moslimani, "Wealth Gaps Across Racial and
      Ethnic Groups," Pew Research Center, December 4, 2023,
      https://www.pewresearch.org/2023/12/04/wealth-gaps-across
      -racial-and-ethnic-groups/.

189   Seventy percent of communities of color: Deloitte, "How Equity
      Can Help Promote Gender Equality in the Workplace," Deloitte
      United Kingdom, 2023, https://www.deloitte.com/uk/en
      /Industries/consumer/blogs/2023/how-equity-can-help
      -promote-gender-equality-in-the-workplace.html.

190   Black consumers spend $910 billion annually: Shelley Stewart,
      "Marketing to the Multifaceted Black Consumer," McKinsey &

Co., May 10, 2022, https://www.mckinsey.com/capabilities
/growth-marketing-and-sales/our-insights/marketing-to-the
-multifaceted-black-consumer.

194 a global value of $126 trillion: Pooneh Baghai et al., "The Great
Reset: North American Asset Management in 2022," McKinsey
& Co., October 2022, https://www.mckinsey.com/~/media
/mckinsey/industries/financial%20services/our%20insights
/the%20great%20reset%20north%20american%20asset%20
management%20in%202022/the-great-reset-north-american
-asset-management-in-2022.pdf, 5.

194 According to the National Association of Investment Companies
(NAIC): "Investment Management: Key Practices Could Provide
More Options for Federal Entities and Opportunities for
Minority- and Women-Owned Asset Managers," GAO-17–726,
United States Government Accountability Office, September
2017, https://www.gao.gov/assets/gao-17–726.pdf.

194 women- and minority-owned firms oversee: "Investment
Management: Key Practices."

194 NAIC research shows: "Examining the Returns 2023:
Further Evidence of Diverse-Owned Private Equity Firm
Outperformance," National Association of Investment Companies,
February 20, 2024, https://naicpe.com/naic-research-and
-reports/examining-the-returns-2023/.

194 McKinsey & Company's 2020 report: Sundiatu Dixon-Fyle,

Kevin Dolan, Dame Vivian Hunt, and Sara Prince, "Diversity Wins: How Inclusion Matters," McKinsey & Company, May 19, 2020, https://www.mckinsey.com/featured-insights/diversity-and-inclusion/diversity-wins-how-inclusion-matters.

194 managers of color are more likely to invest: Boston Consulting Group, "Diversity in Private Investment: A Call to Action for the Industry," Boston Consulting Group, 2024, https://www.bcg.com/publications/2024/diversity-in-private-investment.

196 companies with diverse management teams: Dixon-Fyle, Dolan, Hunt, and Prince, "Diversity Wins."

197 businesses with inclusive cultures: Josh Bersin, "Why Diversity and Inclusion Will Be a Top Priority for 2016," JoshBersin.com, December 7, 2015, https://joshbersin.com/2015/12/why-diversity-and-inclusion-will-be-a-top-priority-for-2016/.

197 "The arc of the moral universe is long": Martin Luther King Jr., "Speech at the Methodist Church," Boston, April 9, 1967, in *The Collected Works of Martin Luther King Jr.*, vol. 4, ed. Peter Holloran (Harper & Row, 1992), 75.

About Robert F. Smith

R OBERT F. SMITH is an American investor, inventor, engineer, philanthropist, and entrepreneur. He is the founder, chairman, and CEO of Vista Equity Partners, which is focused on exclusively investing in enterprise software, data, and technology-enabled businesses. Throughout Smith's life, his commitment to philanthropy and equity has never wavered, and finding ways to make a difference in the communities where he lives and works is central to his character and approach to life. During his 2019 commencement address at Morehouse College, a historically Black college, Smith surprised

the graduating class by pledging to pay off the entire class's student loan debt—a $34 million gift that helped nearly four hundred graduates. He is also a major donor to the National Museum of African American History and Culture, Student Freedom Initiative (SFI), and the Prostate Cancer Foundation, among many others.

About Rev. Dr. Bernice A. King

REV. DR. BERNICE A. KING is a global thought leader, strategist, orator, peace advocate, and CEO of the Martin Luther King Jr. Center for Nonviolent Social Change (The King Center), which was founded by her mother as the official living memorial to the life, work, and legacy of her father. She is a licensed attorney and member of the state bar of Georgia, a certified mediator with the state of Georgia, and a member of Alpha Kappa Alpha Sorority Incorporated. Dr. King holds a doctorate of law from Emory University, a master of divinity from Candler School of Theology at Emory University, and a bachelor's degree in psychology from Spelman College.